Leadership - *It's a* **Marathon**, *Not a* **Sprint**

Everything *you need to know about sustainable achievements*

To Kay

My critical inspiration
to start to run a
Marathon, which then
lead to the book.

love
Gordon

This book is dedicated to Tanya Baldwin, who first inspired me to run the marathon, which in turn gave me the structure for this book.
Thank you, Tanya.

Everything *you need to know*
about sustainable achievements

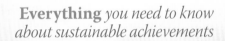

Leadership

It's a **Marathon,** *Not a* **Sprint**

Gordon Tredgold

Leadership - *It's a* **Marathon,** *Not a* **Sprint**

Everything *you need to know about sustainable achievements*

First published in 2013 by

Panoma Press Ltd
48 St Vincent Drive, St Albans, Herts, AL1 5SJ, UK

info@panomapress.com
www.panomapress.com

Book layout by Michael Inns
Artwork by Karen Gladwell
Photographs Carine Cornelis

Printed on acid-free paper from managed forests.

ISBN 978-1-909623-27-9

Contents

Acknowledgements

This book couldn't have been written without the help of so many people; I hope to list them all here but, in reality, all of you cannot fit upon one page...

Carine, my wife: you've supported me without fail. You are my rock and a constant source of inspiration to me.

Angela, my editor and proofreader, whose efforts brought this book to life.

Dave and Tarak, who were there in the cold mornings, running through the craziest of elements in order to help me complete the journey.

Khaled and Mithun, who were constantly encouraging me with my blog, who were two of my first regular readers, and who have reviewed numerous drafts to help this little acorn grow.

Kristen and Simon, who encouraged me to run, who gave great advice and support, and who travelled from the US to run with me in Germany.

Manoj: you ran 100km while I was preparing for my own race, and thus showed me that maybe 42km wasn't that far after all.

Alene, Gisella, Kay and Yolanda: your courage provided me with inspiration and encouragement when the going got tough.

Tade, who gave me lots of writing tips, along with the belief that I could write this book.

Uwe, my right arm at work, and sometimes my left, too: you encouraged me to keep the faith even though many people told me that my ideas wouldn't work in Germany.

Julie, Mark and Phil: you helped provide me with leadership coaching and insight which have helped to mold me into the leader I am today.

Martin, who completed the London Marathon the week before the Dusseldorf Marathon, and whose progress gave me a target to follow.

Everyone who cheered me along each of the 42km… I don't think you realise just how much that helped and how much it meant to me.

Michelle for her help in reviewing this book.

Last but not least, *my parents*, both of whom instiled in me many of the leadership principles which I still hold dear today.

Foreword

Dear Reader

I wonder why you're reading this book... perhaps you're interested in leadership and how that relates to marathon running, or one man's journey towards a heartfelt goal. Maybe it's a yearning for something connected to how your life feels right now, e.g. 'I want more of this' or 'less of that.' Whatever your reason, I'd say you're in a good place to reveal something to yourself, simply by reading the story of someone else. If that sounds like a contradiction, here's what I've found to be true: that when you search for something with a true heart and clear intention, the world will lean and bend around you in order to show you that. All you need to do is hold your clear intention and trust that what you seek is also seeking you. So before you begin to read Gordon's story, please dwell on this thought:

> **What question do I have that I want this book to answer?**

When you have your question, write it down somewhere, and revisit it often. When you answer it, simply ask yourself another question – and begin again.

You'll notice that the story can be read in sequence but it's also possible to read a principle more randomly, e.g. if the idea of the chapter interests you. What's important is that you stay intentional on your own goal for reading the book and in that way the experiences in the book will 'lean and bend' to help surface your own insight. In this way you will see that Gordon's journey is everyone's journey, it's anyone's journey – including yours.

Having watched this story unfold in 'real time' I will say that the impact it has had upon the runner, writer and leader who is Gordon has been huge. Not simply for Gordon but also on the people around him, i.e. in his life and his workplace. What's inspiring is that this came from a simple idea, a small seed of intention that fell upon fertile ground. Namely, through the sheer frustration of not being able to do something to halt his friend's illness, Gordon decided he would do something to prove the presence of possibility where there seemed apparently none. He simply asked himself What can I do? and eventually, unable to resist the heartfelt invitation, the answer arrived. It seems to me that all great notions come from this similar, heartfelt place which is the source of all great truths. So again, I would ask that you become quiet, be still a moment, then ask yourself:

What question do I have that I want this book to answer?

Write your question down; get comfortable and relax into a story of running, of leadership, a classic heroes' journey – which becomes your journey, towards something that you seek... and something that seeks you.

With love and best wishes.

Julie Starr

Introduction

It's been an old dream of mine to write a book. Of course, I didn't know where to start. And the challenge was, to say the least, a daunting one.

To write an *entire* book?

But do you know how to eat an elephant? Bite by bite. So, in August 2012, I decided to start with a blog. I'd write a few things, each and every day, and get a feel for it. Would I enjoy writing? Did I have something to say? And, perhaps most importantly, would anyone else actually be interested? I named my blog *Leadership Principles* and dedicated myself to short blurbs about leadership, writing 300-400 words on whatever subject caught my fancy.

Shortly after I started the blog, a good friend of mine began chemotherapy. Something ignited within me. This was the *seventh* person I knew who had recently undergone cancer treatment. One of my friends, Tanya, contacted me to let me know that her treatment was unsuccessful and that she was dismissing any further medical procedures.

I was so shocked and saddened by all of this news. I wanted to do something. But what? I'm no doctor. I'm not involved in any medical research. But could I support it? I could. I decided I'd try and raise money for a cancer charity. Then there was the question of... *how?*

Then it hit me: I could run a marathon.

I'd never wanted to run a marathon. In fact, one of the things I was most staunchly opposed to in my lifetime was competing in a marathon! Perhaps for that very reason, then, it occurred to me that it was probably the best thing I could do. My friends had been plunged into circumstances they'd never wished for, and they were fighting and prevailing. The least I could do was show some solidarity.

I made my decision in early October 2012, and then I announced to my family and friends that I would be running a marathon within 12 months. Meanwhile, I'd been keeping up with my blog on leadership. As I began my marathon training, I noticed how much my two recent new endeavours – running and writing – correlated.

Many of the leadership values, tactics and strategies which I shared with others were things I could apply to myself during my training. Why not taste my own medicine, then? Why not practise what I preached – and prove its application beyond the business world? The question contorted: no longer did I wonder if I could ever run a marathon; now, *could I lead myself and manage myself as a runner*?

I have structured the book into 26 chapters, each chapter representing one mile of the marathon. Each chapter covers a leadership principle and applies it to my marathon training and professional experience. I've included my progress, tracking how I constantly pushed myself to meet my expectations and goals.

My approach to leadership is founded upon three elements: simplicity, transparency and focus. That is exactly how I wanted to approach the marathon. That is exactly how I would struggle to prevail.

I hope you enjoy my journey!

Big, Bold, Beautiful Goals

"The journey of a thousand miles begins with a single step."

– LAOTZU

What makes a leader? Are true leaders born or made? Are their attributes cultivated over the years, or are they innate? Regardless of how or why people become leaders, the mantle that they then take up is threaded with very specific obligations and responsibilities. One of these responsibilities is to set big, bold goals for their organisations.

But leaders must first know how to lead and challenge themselves – only then can they effectively lead and challenge others in turn. Constantly challenging ourselves is what forces us to improve continuously. As leaders, we need to challenge ourselves and our teams to strive to reach our fullest potential, and to drive the organisation to meet and exceed its limits.

People are as great as you make them out to be. We need to inspire our teams to greatness; this is a major stepping stone in the strategy to success. In particular, *big, bold, beautiful goals.* Small, easily-achieved goals without the vision of big, bold goals are by themselves neither inspiring nor rewarding, when achieved.

When I talk about big, bold goals, I'm talking about quantum leap changes in performance, such as increasing on-time delivery from 30% to over 70%, or reducing operating costs by 30-40% a year without impacting performance, or driving profitability up by 40-50%. The goals could also revolve around something new: launching a new product line, for example, or starting a business in a new market. Your goals could be aspirations, such as becoming *the absolute best* in your field of expertise. As leaders, our job is to ignite the passion within the organisation, to awaken it from its slumber.

Big, bold goals can be as intimidating as they are spectacular, but they don't have to be scary. They may *seem* unachievable, but don't let that daunt you for a second. With careful planning, focus, diligence and commitment, even the most immense of goals can be achieved. That's not to say that we have to aim for the impossible. What I'm implying here is that, contrary to popular belief, the *improbable* is absolutely *possible*.

> *"If your actions inspire others to dream more, learn more, do more, and become more, you are a leader."*
>
> – JOHN QUINCY ADAMS

Such goals can inspire a single person or an entire nation; the beauty of it all is in the inspiration itself. It's also in the glory of the ensuing implementation and achievement of the goal. One of my personal favourites – big and bold on a national scale – is a goal which President John F.

Kennedy announced on 25 May 1961. In front of a special joint session of Congress, he presented a dramatic and ambitious goal: to send an American safely to the moon and back, before the end of the decade. This goal was so inspiring, in fact, that it took on a life of its own; it lived on even after JFK's death, and the big, bold, beautiful goal was achieved in July 1969... before the end of the decade.

The symbolism attached to this incredible goal plays on a very innate and powerful desire of mankind: to keep believing, to keep achieving, and to keep trying despite all odds. Neil Armstrong's "one small step for man; one giant leap for mankind" is not just a play on words. It is an intense and proud declaration. Even the greatest goals are achievable. Even the longest journeys have a beginning and an end.

In light of such examples, isn't anything possible? At one company where I worked, our CEO set a goal that we would work to increase our profitability from 10% to 14% within a four-year period. This was a very big goal indeed, as it meant an increase of 40% in profitability. Most people scoffed at the idea; not everyone believed that this was possible, especially the markets. Our performance had consistently been around the 10% mark for many, many years.

Yet the average profit for companies in our sector was 14%. In fact, some companies were achieving over 20% profit. Therefore, although this was a big, bold goal for us, it wasn't too alarming because it was clear that it was not impossible. There were others who were not only achieving it but who were *exceeding* it.

This is exactly what the team needed. A big, bold, inspiring goal. Having the vision and a sense of direction, we strategised towards the goal. Ultimately, yes, we did increase our profitability by 40%.

Know this: the formula for achieving any goal – no matter how difficult or seemingly inconceivable – is more or less the same. First, you must conceive the dream. With a vision in mind, you know your direction and can map out a path. And thus, it becomes a surmountable goal. The journey towards any goal is called a *plan*. Simplified plans allow us to make progress towards our goals on a daily basis.

- ✓ *Begin the journey.*
- ✓ *Monitor/report the progress.*
- ✓ *Make changes/adjustments as necessary in order to improve.*
- ✓ *Don't give up until you attain the goal.*

If you can strategise the journey to the end result, then you will inspire your team so they can believe that these big goals are achievable. That belief is the most critical cornerstone. Once you've succeeded in inspiring your people, your team will become motivated and the goal will evolve into a self-fulfilling prophecy.

> *Whether you think you can or think you can't, you're usually right.*
>
> – HENRY FORD

One of the biggest and boldest goals that I have been involved with in my career was at a UK telecoms company.

Our instructions were to implement a new solution – one which would normally take 18 months but do it in a period of just *three months*. It was big, bold and pretty scary. But whatever the case, it was our goal.

The solution would require the procurement and installation of new hardware, the installation and configuration of several major software applications (such as SAP), and finally the set-up and test trial of the products which the company wanted to launch. This type of encompassing goal really requires you to challenge the way you normally do things. You're pushed out of your comfort zone, which is the only way you grow. The whole approach requires a fundamental change within the company; it's not possible to simply speed up and expect to reduce the crunch time of a project from 18 months down to three.

So in order to succeed in something like this – to overhaul and revamp your entire system of performance – you need to re-evaluate everything you do. Think about each task, each element. Is it really necessary? Is there a smarter or faster way? To improve, you must challenge your old methods.

That's exactly what we had to do.

To be honest, at the start of this project there were many doubters. Many team members had been involved in similar projects, all of which had taken a minimum of 18 months (some of them even longer!). They'd never before *conceived* of tackling them in merely three months. Yet one of the most interesting aspects of this project was that once we had set this bold goal, and people had overcome the shock of what we were asked to do, the team transitioned into 'solution mode'. As a matter of fact, the very thought of gloriously delivering something at record speed fired us up and forced us to consider what new ways and methods we could implement.

In order to deliver the project, we came up with a simple plan – simple in terms of understanding, that is, since this was a major undertaking. Simplification keeps us sane.

> MONTH 1 - *Install and configure hardware.*
> MONTH 2 - *Install and configure software.*
> MONTH 3 - *Define and test products.*

We then split the overall project team into three teams. Each would focus on one of the key tasks above. All teams had their respective task clear with a concrete deadline. The teams evaluated the processes, judging which procedures were necessary or not. By doing this, many superfluous tasks were eliminated.

Simplification keeps us sane

This alone, however, would not be enough to trim 15 months from a project schedule. There were more challenges to overcome in completing the work within a shorter timeframe. Normally, we'd plan projects around our typical weekly shifts: five days of working eight hours a day. This clearly wouldn't allow for enough time to achieve *this* goal. We therefore came up with aggressive plans in order to meet each deadline: organising the teams so that they worked in non-stop shifts and including long weekend hours.

As the plan began to come together, and as we made more progress, the team could more clearly discern the possibility of success on the horizon. At the start, we monitored progress on a daily basis. We did this to ensure that we were making progress as planned, but also to provide feedback to the other teams that we were on track. It was also a great method to build everyone's momentum. Envisioning success is an *amazing* motivation.

The project was very intense, there was plenty of pressure, and the team worked at an accelerated level. In the end, however, it was worth it: the project was successfully completed and delivered on schedule. As a result, the entire team enjoyed an immense sense of achievement. We had been able to deliver something that usually took 18 months within just three months!

And in the end? Not only had the company set and succeeded at a big, bold, beautiful goal, but we'd also changed the entire company culture, honing our strategy for success. This amazing shift in mentality and focus is possible – not just for an individual, not just for an organisation, but even for an entire nation.

Anything is possible.

"A leader is a dealer in hope."

– NAPOLEON BONAPARTE

Marathon Diary

Big, bold, beautiful goals don't have to be limited to our professional lives. As a matter of fact, they aren't meant to be. They should apply to and appear in all aspects of life. With that in mind, I'm setting a big goal for myself, personally: I've decided that I will run a marathon.

Nope, I've never done this before. My motive? To raise money for charity. My timeframe? The next 12 months. As a 52-year-old who has never run more than five miles at a time – and that was 30 years ago, mind you – this is an *improbable* goal for me.

But not impossible.

Not impossible because I realise that there are many people older than myself – and in worse physical condition, to begin with – who had never run a marathon until the point when they took up running and then completed one! If they could do it, why can't I? Why not anyone?

With this possibility brightening my horizon, I still have to brace myself for reality. Running a marathon is a very big challenge and it requires commitment, planning and determination – *lots* of it. Of course, lots of people don't see it that way. They mistake a difficult challenge for an insurmountable obstacle. Thus, many people have told me that my goal is foolish, that it is impossible, and that I am crazy to consider it (much less attempt it).

But I know that all big, bold, beautiful goals start the same way: create a simple plan. Then start the journey.

Monitor the progress. Report and revise. And keep going till you get it straightened out. First things first, then: I need to create myself a plan! Last week, I researched on the internet and found the Virgin Beginners Marathon Training Plan, which seems reasonable – and doable. Those two characteristics are important. Trust me; seeing the potential in something is quite encouraging.

This is a 144-day training plan, which starts people off from the basics. The first week, all I have to do is run just 15 minutes a day. Even *I* can try and do that! Having helped me achieve those little milestones, the training plan then builds up slowly and gradually towards the ultimate aim: to run a marathon successfully on Day 144.

Coincidently, the local marathon – the Dusseldorf Marathon, held in April – is exactly 180 days away from my starting point.

So now I have my plan: 144 days of training to prepare; then, compete in the Dusseldorf Marathon in April 2013. My first run this week was a 15-minute jog. I completed 1.76 kilometres. A small step, granted.

Yet I already see the significance of this small step, because it is the first one. My goal now seems achievable, if I can just stick to the plan. With my plan in place and my progress underway, the next key element in my strategy is to monitor myself. To do so, I've downloaded an application called *Nike plus*, which runs on the iPhone. *Nike plus* allows me to record daily data (running distances, times, average speeds, etc.) so I can consider and compare.

Even though the goal was improbable before I started, now the goal becomes more probable by the day. Hopefully, it'll become more tangible as the weeks go by. To be successful, I know that I need to focus on what's important and block out anything which distracts me from the goal. For me, it's neither about ground-breaking speed nor record-breaking time. It's simply about completing the distance, running 26 miles (42 kilometres).

Most importantly, what seemed improbable now feels possible.

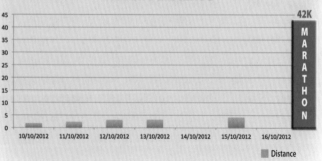

AIM for Success

*The future belongs to those who believe
in the beauty of their dreams.*

– ELEANOR ROOSEVELT

In order to succeed at a particular recipe, you need to include the key ingredients. There's no chicken soup without chicken, is there? You can't call your drink a café latte if there's no milk in it, can you? And a chocolate chip cookie simply does not exist without chocolate. Just so, when you AIM for success, your recipe will produce outstanding results if you've included the correct ingredients:

A*spiration*

I*nspiration*

M*otivation*

In order to succeed, we must ensure that we are fully aligned with our goals. We must be committed to them. That also means that we must be prepared to go the extra mile when the going gets tough and when it would just be easier to quit. Sometimes the winner succeeds simply because he refuses to quit.

Let's enter the world of boxing for a moment…

Many fighters join the game because they see it as an escape: a way out of poverty, a way out of the ghetto, a way to make good money. Their aspiration is short-sighted and simple: make money, get rich and get out. A short-sighted aspiration, however, leads to a short-sighted career. You may have heard of some world champions who lose their drive once they have achieved their primary goal of becoming a millionaire. Then they no longer have the motivation to train and to sweat in the gym in order to win that next fight. They lose their edge, they fail to maintain their level of performance, and they succumb to defeat. They either lose or they simply do not fight again.

Now take the champions who had a different sort of aspiration: the ones who desired to be amongst the world's greatest boxers – say, to be the undefeated world champion. This is an aspiration that requires constant work and constant improvement – and there is always room for self-improvement. For Julio Cesar Chavez, boxing was a way of life. He fought 116 times and triumphed 108. He won six world titles at three different weights. If he'd been in it just for the money or the freedom, he'd never have made it so far. It probably was his aspiration to be *great* that burned within him, and this allowed for both the inspiration and the motivation.

> *"An arrow can only be shot by pulling it backward. When you feel like you are being dragged back by difficulties, it means that you are torqueing up to launch forward."*
>
> – ANONYMOUS

More often than not, lack of motivation is the classic excuse for why we don't meet our goals. Speaking from personal experience, however, I believe the issue is not about motivation – or, rather, the lack thereof – that impacts our ability to achieve. I believe it goes much deeper than that.

It might be the lack of alignment between our desires, our aspirations and our goals. It could be that we lack belief in our ability. It could even mean that we are just not inspired. Yet these three ingredients are intrinsic to the recipe; anything less makes for something less. Think of these as the three spices which will fire us up to achieve.

Aspiration goes first into the melting pot. In order to influence people, you must first understand them – their desires, their needs, their dreams. What do they aspire to? You might not ever get a chance to find out what people's true individual aspirations are – that they want to be a rock star, or a heavyweight boxing champion, a worthier parent, a millionaire, a skydiving instructor – but you already know one innate human desire which they have, because it's one that you share with them. Ultimately, we all desire to be happy, healthy and loved. We all desire importance – the feeling of being worthy, of being *valued.*

We all want to 'be somebody'.

Thus, you can empathise with mankind's most important desire: to be valued, to feel worthy, to feel that we've done a good day's work and that we have contributed. Once you understand and accept this about people, you can ignite that aspiration – *I want to achieve, I want to contribute, I want to be worthy, I want to be great!* – by inspiring them. Once you establish the aspiration, it must then be encouraged by ***inspiration***.

How do you inspire others? How do you 'create' inspiration? Well, what better way than by envisioning the ideal? An inspiration is a vision – a vision of success. The vision must be tangible. It must be built upon a foundation of reality, so the stepping stones need to be realistic and appropriate. What would success look like? What would success feel like? How would a particular individual feel when successful?

Show your team how success is achievable.

Provide people with a realistic plan, arm them with the right tools and resources, and build the belief that the goal can be accomplished. Creating the vision is relatively easy. The hardest part is in instiling the *belief* that success is something attainable. You need to overcome the obstacles of people's doubts, their lack of confidence, or perhaps even a previous track record of underachievement.

Once you have added a healthy dose of *inspiration* – a compelling vision with strong belief that it can be achieved – then you need to mix in the ***motivation***...

How does this third ingredient come into play? Motivation is typically instiled by tracking, showing and celebrating the progress made towards a goal. Monitoring the progress reinforces the belief that success is possible, which in turn skyrockets the inspiration. Keep in mind that merely monitoring progress is often not enough. In addition to showing progress, you need to recognise and reward it. The act of recognition cultivates the feeling of value – that the work pays off, that this is a good job – and this then turns and feeds our aspirations.

> *"Do not lose hold of your dreams or aspirations. For if you do, you may still exist but you have ceased to live."*
>
> – HENRY DAVID THOREAU

Just as in any recipe, remember, the quantity and the timing of the ingredients matter. Each ingredient complements the other two; all together, they make a brilliant recipe. Aspiration is the most important; without it, you have nothing to strive towards. Inspiration is the most difficult to concoct. Finally, provided you already have aspiration and inspiration, motivation is the easiest to add.

But, you might point out, it's easy to *lose* motivation, too, isn't it? True. This is why, if the aspiration and the inspiration aren't already aligned, the alchemy goes awry. The last ingredient will be lacking or dwindling. So fan the fires and keep that motivation burning. You'll derive it from the feeling that comes from progressing towards your goal. It encourages you, but it's also a reward for the progress made.

Let's take a look at how the team of Manchester United handled this.

When Alex Ferguson took over as manager, this football team had not won the championship title for over 20 years. Did that matter to Ferguson? Not really. His goal – his aspiration – actually went far beyond that. He did not want them to *just* win the championship. What he wanted to do was to knock Liverpool off their perch as the leader of English football. Since Liverpool had won the championship 12 more times than Manchester had, this was something of a tall order. Improbable, but not impossible.

That was Ferguson's – and thus Manchester United's – big, bold, beautiful goal.

Turns out, not only did the team recruit a good manager, but they'd hired a man whose goals were completely aligned with those of the club. Both wanted the team to achieve long-term sustainable success, one that would leave a name and a legacy. When Ferguson recruited players for Manchester, he looked for one dominant quality: talented players *who put the club first.* In fact, he sold the players who considered themselves bigger and more important as individual players than as team players. He sold the ones who thought that one championship win was enough. And he replaced them with people who were armed with his type of aspiration.

Ferguson not only had the aspiration to make Manchester the top team in English football, he also had the strong belief that he would succeed. Prior to joining Manchester, Ferguson had coached an unfashionable team, Aberdeen, to winning both domestic and European triumphs, including a final victory over Real Madrid. Having achieved this difficult undertaking at Aberdeen, Ferguson had the perfect credentials to convince the Manchester players that he could lead them; he thus provided inspiration. As a leader of football players, of men, Ferguson was also able to provide the final ingredient: motivation.

Ferguson achieved his goal of knocking down Liverpool. He also became the most successful manager in football history, and made Manchester the most successful team in England. His trophies included: Champions League (2), Premier League (13), FA Cup (5), League Cup (4), Club World Cup (1), Intercontinental Cup (1), Cup Winners' Cup (2) European Super Cup (2), Community Shield (9), Scottish Premier League (3), Scottish Cup (4), Scottish League Cup (1), and Scottish First Division (1).

The strategy is straightforward: create alignment between the aspiration and the goal; find the appropriate inspiration; and create some progress to generate motivation. If you can similarly realise the importance of Aspiration, Inspiration, and Motivation, and how these three elements interact and influence each other, you can master the recipe.

It's common sense, in a way. Your probability to succeed is far better if you realise what you're aiming at.

"It concerns us to know the purposes we seek [...] for then, like archers aiming at a definite mark, we shall be more likely to attain what we want."

– ARISTOTLE

Marathon Diary

I've always been pretty athletic. I played rugby competitively for over three decades, from the age of nine. I represented my schools in a variety of sports including rugby, football, cricket, swimming, table tennis and badminton. Nevertheless, I used to joke with people that one of my goals in life was never to run a marathon.

Not that I hadn't been asked to. Running a marathon was all the rage in the '80s, but I resisted. I simply couldn't see the point in running 26 miles. It seemed to be an awful lot of effort with no valuable purpose. My friends would argue against that, telling me: "If you do it, then you could always say, '*I ran a marathon!*'" *Big deal*, I thought. *Who cares if I run a marathon?*

Why am I so keen now, suddenly, to run a marathon?

It began in 2009. That's the year when I found out that a significant number of my friends and colleagues had been diagnosed with cancer. Unfortunately, these cancer-stricken individuals seem to be increasing in number, and I'm powerless to stop that. But this changed my entire perspective about the marathon. I realised that I could at least show my support by running a marathon. I would take on a fight I didn't have to fight (overcoming my distaste and inability to run a marathon). And by participating, I would raise money for cancer charity. A lot of people actually do this.

It isn't really about running. At the heart of it, it's

a matter of solidarity and contribution. Competing in this marathon is my aspiration.

When I decided on the marathon, a little voice buzzed around in my head: *But you don't* want *to run a marathon! One of your life goals is never to run a marathon!* Then there were the doubts. Could I even really run a marathon, given my age and physical condition? I haven't run in… a while.

I shut up these thoughts by realising this: my friends hadn't asked for cancer. They didn't *want* it. They didn't want to go through chemotherapy. They didn't want this challenge in their lives. But they had no choice. And they are my inspiration. If *they* can put themselves through chemo, then *I* can put myself through a training regime which will prepare me to run this marathon and complete it.

What is my problem? That I don't want to run a marathon? It's the least I can do.

Let me add something else. Fauja Singh became the oldest marathon runner in the world. Can you guess how old he was? *100 years old.* If he could do it, then so can I. (Did you hear that whooshing noise? My excuses just flew out of the window.) It isn't like I'm aiming to win the Gold at the Olympics. My goal is to cross the finish line in order to raise some money.

And once I really take a good look around, my sources of inspiration seem unlimited…

Kristen, a friend's wife, emerged successfully from chemotherapy and decided to take control of her life. She defined herself as *marathon woman* rather than *cancer survivor woman.* I'm proud to say that she's since run *nine* marathons. She's told me that if I compete in April, she'll come and run with me to support me. And she's not the only one; there's Alene, Tanya, Kay, Gisella, and many more –all of whom have won or are fighting their way to health.

I've also found sources of motivation. I've been hearing this from many friends: *OK, if you're going to do it then we will join and train with you*. It is no longer just my battle. I have allies. And this week, as I follow the training plan, I am becoming more comfortable with running. My endurance is increasing. 15-minute jogs have expanded to 20-30 minutes. Progress may look slow now, but the point is to get into a routine of running regularly (four to six times a week).

I love progressing in line with the plan. It gives me the confidence that I can succeed. By the end of the week, I've increased my running time to an hour a day! I posted my progress online, which has led to a lot of support and encouragement from folks who are checking in on me.

Believe it or not, I think I might enjoy this…

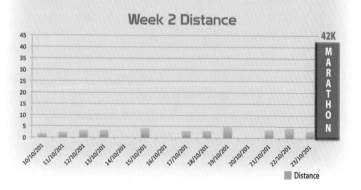

Week 2 Distance

The Power of Why

> *"The will to win means nothing without the will to prepare."*
>
> – JUMA IKANGAA

Understanding the reason *why* you do things – the explanation of any riddle – gives you the power of knowledge. Knowing *why* gives you the edge you need to improve the probability of success. If people don't know why they are doing something, then they can't understand its importance and why it is beneficial. They don't know why they *need* to do it.

When my son Dan was 16, he decided that he was going to be a professional musician, a guitarist in fact. He knew that in order to be a professional musician he would need to go to music college, and the only way to get into his first-choice music college would be if he was a Grade 8 guitarist. He also knew that to achieve the required level he was going to have to practise, practise, practise.

This gave him a great sense of purpose; it drove him to practise 4 hours per day over the next 2 years until he finally passed the Grade 8 guitarist exam. Dan knew exactly why he was practising; it was the difference between achieving his dream or not, and this why is a very powerful motivator.

We all parallel this mentality; if you and your team understand *why* you need to do something, this gives you a sense of purpose. You'll all be motivated to succeed. Mind you, this is not about just knowing what you are doing for a project that needs to be completed by the end of the year. It goes deeper than that. If you can identify the higher purpose of your work, and if you can communicate that to the team, the team will be prepared to go the extra mile in order to achieve success *because they understand why it's important.*

Is there a difference between *aspiration* and *the power of why*?

Yes. There is a degree of overlap, but there is a subtle difference, too. The way I see it, our aspiration is based on our *want* to do something, whereas the power of 'why' is backed by why we *need* to do something, especially if that something has been requested of us by someone else. An overlap, for example, is when the leader's *why* becomes the entire team's aspiration.

> *"Vision without action is a daydream.*
> *Action without vision is a nightmare."*
>
> – JAPANESE PROVERB

A few years ago, I worked for a parcel delivery firm. One of our projects was to improve on-time delivery. I'd been involved in a similar sort of project before, and honestly, most people (myself included) would have preferred to be involved with something 'more interesting'. It would be fair to say that, as a result, ours wasn't what you'd call a highly motivated team.

When we started the project, the business project manager called for a meeting. He said that he wanted to explain *why* this project was important. He chose a very interesting approach. He began by asking us for the reasons why we thought this project was important. We said:

- ✓ *In order to reduce costs…*
- ✓ *To increase customer satisfaction…*
- ✓ *To increase market share…*
- ✓ *To reduce the penalties we have to pay when parcels are delivered late…*

To each of these, his answer was "No, guess again." Finally, after about 30 minutes of processing incorrect answers, he interrupted us:

"OK, I will tell you why this project is important. The purpose of the project is to improve the on-time delivery of parcels to our customers. This is very important because it's the only way we can ensure that children receive the birthday presents which are sent to them *on their birthdays*, not the day after or the week after. There is no Santa Claus. That's *our* mission. It's our job to ensure that Christmas presents sent through us are delivered on time, on or before Christmas day, and not after.

"Apart from the children, we need to think of those who are ill. They depend on *us*. There are thousands of people who receive medication which is delivered by us, and we have to ensure that we deliver that medication on time. They have to have it when they need it, and thus we minimise their suffering. We could be saving lives... or are we doing the opposite? This is why this project is important. All of these people depend on us. And we don't want to let them down."

The team were dumbfounded. We'd never looked at the project in *this* light. Once we saw the real reasons behind *why* we were supposed to be doing what we were doing, we became intensely motivated. We could see why the job was important and what the benefits were. Not just individual reasons or professional reasons for the company's own good. First and foremost, for our customers.

Our boss gave us an incredible sense of purpose. Suddenly, this wasn't just another project (or worse, a nuisance). We were working on a very important and symbolic project, and we *wanted* to be a part of it. Things were not only delivered on time, but actually ahead of schedule. People put in extra effort in order to ensure that we succeeded. And we did!

Now whenever I have a large task that my teams need to undertake, I try to identify what the bigger purpose is first. It's my job to communicate to the team and show them *why* we need to do what we do. Persuading someone to want something is the best way to involve them and motivate them.

"The important thing is that men should have purpose in life. It should be something useful, something good."

– DALAI LAMA

Marathon Diary

I no longer ever stop to wonder *Why have I taken on this goal? Why am I training to compete in this marathon?* I've resolved the question to that 'why' from the moment that I decided to compete, because my action was driven by my desire. The answer is clear and simple: I *want* to show solidarity for my friends who are going through chemo and who are fighting cancer. I *want* to contribute financially to support cancer sufferers. I *want* to help.

This gives me a great sense of purpose. It's the powerful push that gets me out of bed six days a week at 6am to go and run.

I read quite a bit about running marathons. Ironically enough, most of the authors say that you need to know *why* you're running a marathon. The purpose is important, but not all purposes are created equal. For example, if you're training just to lose weight or to get fit, then the odds are you will give up. The process is too intense, and it requires an equally intense reason. I can certainly believe that.

It isn't always easy. Some days I feel tired. Sometimes I don't feel motivated. Often I'm running all alone, and that's not usually fun. The training itself is no piece of cake (most training plans require you to run five or six days a week, for at least a six-month period). But it makes sense, because the race itself is hard. In order to run 26 miles, you need to be physically, mentally and emotionally prepared.

But I feel lucky. I have a very strong purpose, and I am clear about why I want to do this. I believe that I can. So I never feel like I am *really* running alone.

I always feel that my friends and supporters are running with me – in spirit at least, if not in body. I injured my foot playing squash this week, and that stopped my training for four days... but it didn't prevent me from completing a major milestone. I ran a 5K for the first time.

This doesn't mean that there aren't days when I think *I don't want to run today,* because there are. But I do it anyway.

Here's another strong reason for me to follow through with my training: if I want to complete the race and not look like a fool, I need to have the capability and the confidence that will drive me to the finish line. I know my current fitness level won't allow me to complete a half marathon, let alone a full marathon (this became very clear to me when I puffed and panted my way through my first 15-minute run and thought I was going to die). I need to be running six days a week. I need to increase the distances that I am running and the duration of the runs. I need to improve my cardiovascular fitness, my endurance, and my mental strength in order to be able to complete the race successfully.

It is clear to me what has to be done and why.

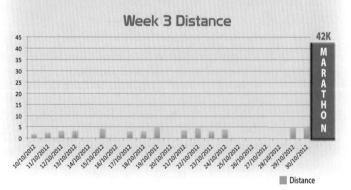

Week 3 Distance

MILE FOUR...

Defining Success

> *"When a man feels throbbing within him the power to do what he undertakes as well as it can possibly be done, this is happiness, this is success."*

– ORISON SWETT MARDEN

If you don't know what success looks like, how will you know when you have achieved it? Success breeds success, but it's easier to cultivate a tree when you know what kind of seed you've sown. It's essential that you know what to look for, otherwise perhaps you won't be able to recognise it even if it stares you in the face. Or maybe you will just stop short of the finishing line with success just within your grasp.

When JFK set his ambitious goal, he clearly defined what success was. His goal wasn't merely to land on the moon; he'd defined the specifics: to land a man on the moon and bring him back safely before the end of the decade. A clearly defined goal communicates to everyone what is needed in order to cross the finish line. It lays out what criteria need to be met before the champagne corks can be popped and the celebration begun.

How do *you* define your success to others? You must define it for yourself, of course, before you can share any sort of definition. That holds true in the social as well as in the professional spheres of life. If I don't know what success looks like for you, how will I be able to say *well done*, or congratulate you on your success, or give you reward and recognition or feedback for improvement? How could you do the same for me, providing quality work and 'succeeding', if you don't know my standards?

If we can concur with our business partners and with our teams about what success looks like, we will have clear agreement on when we will be able to declare victory. If we're not yet at that agreed-upon 'finish line', we can come up with a strategy with which to get there, having a shared and recognisable goal in sight. Once we've done that, we know where we're headed and what path we've got to take in order to get there. Such a map significantly increases our probability of succeeding.

It's pretty basic:

✓ *Define success.*
✓ *Set up a strategy.*

Knowing that success is probable and imminent is motivating. What's even better is enjoying regular tastes of success along the way! Once we can agree on what success looks like, and once we outline a path to get there and achieve our goal, we can celebrate our stepping stone successes. Motivation and momentum help to cultivate a *Winning Culture.* This propels us faster towards success – and makes the journey more positive and enjoyable.

"A leader takes people where they want to go. A great leader takes people where they don't necessarily want to go, but ought to be."

– ROSALYNN CARTER

To do this, *you* need to identify the intermediate successes on the route to your team's ultimate success. These are the aforementioned tastes of victory – the delicious bites and whiffs that get your mouth watering while you're cooking up that recipe for the ultimate success.

These small milestones need to be *meaningful but achievable*.

Here is an example of the improvement process that my team went through in order to completely revamp our company's operational IT performance. Originally, we didn't have any performance measurements in place, so our goal was twofold: first, we had to actually implement the new measurements; second, we then needed to increase our performance until we hit our desired level.

Here are the *Steps for Success* which we first had to identify very clearly:

> STEP 1 - **Measure monthly performance.**
>
> STEP 2 - **Achieve top performance in a single month.**
>
> STEP 3 - **Achieve top performance for three months in a row.**
>
> STEP 4 - **Achieve 80% top performance for full year.**
>
> STEP 5 - **Achieve 90% top performance for full year.**

Looking at this, most people are probably thinking that Steps 1-3 are nothing to shout about. But in order to arrive at Step 5, those earlier steps are essential. And ironically, despite their being 'nothing to shout about', many people never get past them! Our doing so, then, was certainly something to celebrate. With each step clearly defined, we knew when and how we accomplished each small goal. With each accomplishment, there was some degree of reward and recognition. Simultaneously, we raised the bar a little higher.

At Step 1, we defined what success would look like and we began to measure ourselves against it. During Step 2, we proved to ourselves that we could achieve success at least once. That is an important milestone, because this first achievement is what generates belief. With Step 3, we showed that we could repeat that pattern of success (sustainable success). By Step 4, we were striving for a high consistency of performance.

Thus, by clearly defining success from the very beginning, the teams came up with a plan to achieve the targets. I was able to motivate them by celebrating their early successes, and this all led to a situation where success bred success. Ultimately, we not only achieved Step 5 – we surpassed it.

Once your team tastes victory, it will want to taste it again and again. We humans are brilliantly ambitious that way. Don't be surprised if your teams themselves come up with ideas on how to raise the bar even higher, and achieve even more success.

Success is deliciously addictive.

"Always bear in mind that your own resolution to success is more important than any other one thing."

– ABRAHAM LINCOLN

Marathon Diary

When it comes to my Marathon Goal, I've had to define what success means to me. As an unfit 52-year-old who was never much of a runner, I want to keep it simple. I don't want to be too ambitious. I want a fathomable goal, reasonable for a guy in my own shoes.

Success right now means this: complete the marathon and raise some money for charity. *Not* win the marathon and then head straight to the next summer Olympics. *Not* break the record for fastest marathon runner in the world. Just train, get fit, get started, get done, and support my friends. For someone who has never run a marathon – who isn't even a regular jogger – just surviving to the end is big and bold enough, if not beautiful.

The Dusseldorf Marathon has a cut-off time of five hours and 30 minutes, so I need to complete it within that timeframe and still be alive. That's good enough for me. That will be a job well done. Then celebrations can commence!

Now, I need to focus. As a naturally competitive person, I'm already considering what would be a good finishing time for me. Yes, I realise that running a marathon is not something that most people would even dream of tackling, and anything beyond that, therefore, would be a bonus. Still, I don't want to come out last.

I keep reminding myself of the fable of the Tortoise and the Hare. Shooting off ahead and feeling oh-so-sure of himself, the Hare thinks that he can afford a nap amidst all his sprinting and showing off. He oversleeps, of course, and wakes to discover that he's lost the race to the Tortoise.

I keep telling myself that I am the Tortoise: *Be slow, but steady – don't rush off like a fool only to fail in the end. The Tortoise gets to the finish line. Be the Tortoise!*

My training plan takes 26 weeks to complete; when I decided to compete, the marathon was over 30 weeks away, so I knew then that I needed to create some small intermediate goals to motivate and encourage me along the way.

Here's what I've come up with:

- ✓ **Goal 1 – Run five times a week**, no matter how far, how fast, or how long; just get into the rhythm of running regularly.

- ✓ **Goal 2 – Complete a 5K without stopping**; start to build some stamina.

- ✓ **Goal 3 – Run a 5K in under 30 minutes**; meet a benchmark to show improvements in speed and stamina (both of which are critical for completing the marathon).

✓ **Goal 5 – Run a 10K without stopping**; complete a quarter of the ultimate distance.

✓ **Goal 6 – Run a 10K in under one hour**; using this timeframe as a reference point, this will provide me with the confidence that finishing within five and a half hours is possible

✓ **Goal 7 – Run half a marathon**: 13.1 miles or 21 kilometres; a significant milestone which will prove that I really am well on my way.

I'm at the point where I can run a 5K in under 30 minutes. According to my plan, this will become my regular training distance for the next few weeks, and hopefully this will show me the progress that I'm making. As I complete each goal, my motivation and confidence grow. 'Running a marathon' has transitioned from *impossible dream* to *probable accomplishment*. As I share my progress of clearing these hurdles and receive the feedback of my friends, I see that their doubts also begin to evaporate and they, too, are slowly beginning to believe.

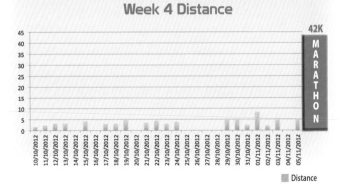

Week 4 Distance

MILE FOUR - *Defining Success*

MILE FIVE . . .

When to Involve the Troops

"Sticks in a bundle are unbreakable."

– KENYAN PROVERB

When you're fighting a battle, how long do you have to fight it alone? What's a duel, and what's a war? When should you call for reinforcements? When can you expect to find an army at your back? Someone asked me the question: *At what point do we need to involve more people – like experts – when we're shooting for those big goals?*

This is an interesting and difficult question to answer. I see it as a very tough balancing act that we have to get right.

If you involve too many people too early, then your goals run the risk of becoming tempered and watered down. On the other hand, if you involve too few people or involve them too late, people might feel excluded and this can then lead to resistance, tension and lack of commitment. That can be a huge source of conflict.

In my opinion, the team defining the objectives and the goals needs to be small. And by *small*, I mean perhaps one to two people.

I'll explain why I'm so conservative with that number. The more people you have involved in defining the goal, the more reasons they'll provide you as to why you cannot hit your target. (It's more 'natural' to think initially of what could go wrong. Remember when someone turned up late for a date or a meeting. A dozen bad scenarios probably ran through your head – from *he doesn't like me anymore* to *maybe he got into a car crash.* Turned out, he'd just stopped to fill up with petrol.) If there are too many people involved, your goal will be watered down from *big, bold and beautiful* to *small and not-so-impressive.* It's nobody's fault, *per se*; it's just the way of people, for there are as many opinions as there are voices. In the end, it's your decision, and your voice has to make the choice.

We need to be dedicated and fearless when setting big and ambitious goals, and this is more easily done if we only have to deal with (or convince) a small group. Large groups tend to be more cautious, argumentative, and often lean towards the safe side – not what you need when setting big, bold goals. You need healthy doses of risk and ambition and creativity, and those characteristics can get trampled by the masses.

I've experienced this in the workplace time and time again, like that time when I set one company's goal for an on-time delivery increase to 80% (as compared to our old average performance of 35%). If I had consulted with a larger group, I am sure we would have tempered the goal and probably set it at 60%; 80% wouldn't have even been considered, much less reached.

In my opinion, keep the team to a minimum when you're at the first step of defining success and setting the goals for a change.

So then, the second step. You have to define the *why* behind the *what*; why this goal is important, what the benefits are, the reasons behind it, and so forth. The more inspirational the goal, the more convincing your *why* – and the bigger the buy-in.

This is when more people begin to show up.

As soon as *what* and *why* have been defined, you can begin gathering an army to tackle *how.* Remember this: the goal is non-negotiable now. There will be those who will try to deter you from it. There will be those who won't be able to fathom the big picture. But the team's focus should be on brainstorming and mapping out *the road* to success. The vision of success has already been taken care of. All the energy must now be channelled to discovering how to achieve the bold goals – not how to temper or reset them.

The Three Key Principles to Driving Change

✓ *Define the problem (the goal) with as few people as possible.*

✓ *Create an important and inspiring reason that people can buy into.*

✓ *Define the solution (the strategy for success while involving and welcoming more people (the troops).*

There will always be some resistance, of course. You need to see beyond that now. The Chinese have a popular proverb: *It is better to light the candle than to curse the darkness.* Problems exist to be solved. Your vision must be powerful enough, and your focus must be just as keen.

Don't ask your team: *Why shouldn't we do this?* Instead, ask your team: *Tell me what you need to make this happen.*

If you can attain the balance, your larger group will not feel excluded. Instead, those people will feel involved. They will take up the challenge and work with you to define the solution. After all, the resulting solution will be their brainchild, too, and involvement breeds commitment. Thus do we set big, bold, challenging goals, while inspiring people and ensuring their commitment.

> *"Never tell people how to do things. Tell them what to do and they will surprise you with their ingenuity."*
>
> – GEORGE PATTON

Marathon Diary

Running a marathon was never something I'd wanted to do, so it wasn't my first choice. Remember that I've never considered myself a runner, I didn't want to run one, and I wasn't even sure whether it was possible for me.

Nevertheless, I finally decided that running a marathon is actually a good goal. My brainstorming team for defining the goal was small: I asked one of my friends, Tanya, what she thought about the idea and she told me that it definitely encouraged her and that she thought it was a nice gesture towards our friends who were fighting cancer.

So that was it. I was going to run a *Marathon*.

I didn't know how I'd manage it, or whether it *was* really possible, but I knew I wanted to do it. And that's what I'm fighting for this week, training and sweating and pounding away on the streets. Because I felt that this was going to be a difficult process, I also decided to announce my commitment before I had too much time to think about it and back out.

That's what you could call *calling in the big guns*.

I didn't discuss this with my wife or any of my other friends whom I thought might try to dissuade me. I just announced it. Publically. I chose a channel that would reach many people at once – I updated my status on Facebook:

> *Given that I have too many friends who are either going through, have gone through, or are about to start chemotherapy, I have decided I want to do something to help. I am committing to running a marathon within the next 12 months in order to raise money for cancer charity, to try and help and to show my support.*

Wow! A lot of people suddenly noticed. And… I was stuck. I had no choice but to follow through on my word. My big, bold, beautiful goal was public. My commitment was made. Furthermore, as soon as I posted that up, people started responding. *Are you crazy?… Why not go for 10K, a 10K run is doable, you're not a runner. This will be very, very tough!... At least limit it to just a half marathon, but not a full marathon... It's too much, you're not fit enough! You will never be able to do it... my boss told me 'this will end in tears'...*

Whew.

The weight of doubt and resistance from others was intense, but I had already announced it and I was committed. If I had decided to discuss this with my wife and close friends before making the commitment, I know they would have talked me out of it – with the best intentions, of course, because they didn't want me to risk my health or time or energy on something so hard. At least, they would have tried to persuade me otherwise: to do something easier (such as a 10K run) or raise money for charity some other way.

I did not wish to be persuaded otherwise.

Then it started to get interesting. Ironically enough, after the initial resistance and doubts, and as people realise that I am fully committed and won't change my goal, things change. Instead of being doubtful and concerned, these folks have transformed into a supportive team. Instead of posting negativity, they're spreading positivity. I've been getting a lot of great feedback and suggestions as to how I'll be able to train and compete!

Suddenly these people are in solution mode, not resistance mode.

My wife Carine also changed her mind. "If you're going to do this, then you need to start drinking more water and eating healthier meals; I will take care of that. I will book you into a Pilates class too, as you're going to need to do some stretching to help you with your running. Also, if you're going to run four to six times a week, we will need to buy you some more kit, especially for running outside when it's cold." She's the best!

Then there's my best friend Dave, who has bought me the *Nike plus* running application. This invaluable tool allows me to measure and track my performance. He's also found a running coach who gives great tips on running technique and training regimes. This is exactly what I need from my team: support and solutions on how to achieve my goal. By involving them at the right time, I've ensured that we are able to focus on the *how*, and not challenge the *what*.

In other news, regularly running 5km, I was tempted to push myself a little further to see whether I could complete 10km. This is another significant milestone for me. I managed to do this on the 10th of November, exactly one month after starting my training. Very encouraging! I'm right on track!

Week 5 Distance

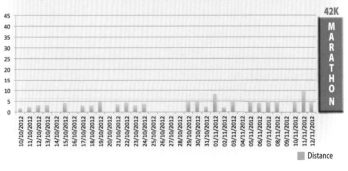

MILE FIVE - *When to Involve the Troops*

The Importance of the First Followers

"Every leader needs to look back once in a while to make sure he has followers."

– ANONYMOUS

If a ship is nothing without its captain, the captain is nothing without his first mate. The first followers, the first disciples, the first mate – however you choose to term these individuals – are essential. Imagine how much power and confidence such a person can provide. Apart from likely being your right hand throughout the entire process, these people are the first to believe your idea might just work.

Suddenly, through someone else's support, you've got credibility. You make sense to someone. You're an inspiration. You already believe in yourself, which is necessary; now you've got somebody else who believes in you and your vision, which is wonderful.

Do you know of Bayard Rustin? Maybe. Maybe not. But I'm certain that you've heard of Martin Luther King, Jr.

Many people are not aware of the role Bayard Rustin played in the social movement for civil rights. He was a passionate advocate and a leading activist for civil rights, gay rights, socialism, and pacifism.

A master strategist and tireless activist, Bayard Rustin is best remembered as the organizer of the 1963 March on Washington, one of the largest nonviolent protests ever held in the United States.

He brought Gandhi's protest techniques to the American civil rights movement, and helped mold Martin Luther King, Jr. into an international symbol of peace and nonviolence.

In February 1956, when Bayard Rustin arrived in Montgomery to assist with the nascent bus boycott, Martin Luther King, Jr. had not personally embraced nonviolence.

In fact, there were guns inside King's house, and armed guards posted at his doors. Rustin persuaded boycott leaders to adopt complete nonviolence, teaching them Gandhian nonviolent direct protest.

> *"No man is a leader until his appointment is ratified in the hearts and minds of men."*
>
> – ANONYMOUS

First followers are often not as visible as the leaders. They're often the ones cheering on the sidelines, the ones dedicated to brainstorming and encouraging, the squires who meticulously prepare and polish before their jousting knight grasps his lance and goes thundering across the field to victory. But can you envision Batman without

Robin? Would Don Quixote have survived without Sancho Panza? Frodo had the ring and the glory, yet he couldn't have completed his journey to Mordor without Sam. Would Robin Hood have gained such a large band of merry men if Little John had not stepped forward first? Several great presidents and leaders of the world could not have fulfilled their dreams without the support of their spouses.

Irish singer Bob Geldof – 'the man behind Live Aid' – wasn't the only man behind that pop charity band. He certainly couldn't have accomplished all that he'd set out to do without his first follower.

Geldof chose his first followers wisely, including enlisting the help of Scottish guitarist, singer and songwriter James 'Midge' Ure (from the group Ultravox) to help produce a charity record. Taking Geldof's original lyrics, Midge composed the remainder of the songs, and also created the melody and backing track for the record. Ure even stepped up to fulfil the production duties, jointly setting up the Band Aid Trust with Geldof in 1984. Their Live Aid concerts raised more than $50 million for African famine relief.

The first follower is often your greatest source of motivation. This person increases your confidence that you are on the right track. As we've discussed before, such a belief tends to become a self-fuelling cycle and a self- fulfilling prophecy of success. As a result, you gain more confidence and you attract even more followers.

A great idea must be born... and must be recognised. Only then may it come at last into fruition.

"To lead the people,
walk behind them."

– LAO TZU

Marathon Diary

My first follower was my best friend Dave.

"If you're going to do this," he said, "then I will do it with you."

What more could I ever ask for? He never said *this is crazy*. He was just, *OK let's do it*. He became my first follower, blessing my mission with credibility. I don't feel like some deranged idiot who has let his imagination set an impossible goal. Once we both agreed on the logic of the goal, it seemed far less daunting and dubious.

Dave gives me confidence, encouragement, and much-needed support. It's not always easy to get up every morning and go running, but now I have some support and also a bit of peer pressure, with neither of us wanting to miss a run. Then guess what? Shortly after Dave started to run with me, our friend Tarak also joined in the training; after a couple of runs, he said would also go for the marathon.

Now there are almost always three or four of us running together!

As more and more people see that I am running, they too have decided that they will take up running. Not necessarily to compete in a marathon, of course, but they are still inspired to improve their general fitness and well-being. As this began to snowball, a couple of friends in the US, both of them marathon runners, contacted me: "If you're serious, then we will come over and run it with you." They'd cross country borders! This is not only a big commitment from them, but it also increases my own personal level of commitment. And there's great strength in numbers.

No way am I letting them down after that. Now I *have* to do it, which is additional motivation for me. But the most powerful catalyst of all is still: *I want to.*

The news that a couple of old school friends are coming from the US to run with me has triggered another round of voluntary recruitment, with my sister and two daughters deciding that they, too, will take up running. My daughters Jessica and Lucy are only 16 and 14 respectively, too young to take on the full marathon. However, given that they are very keen and have even started running early in the morning, this has given me great encouragement.

This week I've been running a mix of 5km and 10km runs. I feel like I'm really getting into the swing of it. Running regularly, five or six times a week, and making good progress with the distances. Another major milestone has been achieved: I ran my last 10K of the week in under an hour! This was a great goal to achieve, but I need to remember to maintain my focus. The goal is to run the marathon, not complete the fastest 10K possible. There are many more kilometres to go.

I have had my share of professional success as a leader in the business world, but I've never thought of myself as a leader in my private social sphere. I never considered my ability to inspire others to do anything like this. I hadn't predicted running to challenge my mind and body with a marathon.

It all started with one follower. Dave joined me first. He added credibility to the dream, and he helped me morph it into a tangible goal. A group goal, a team effort. Otherwise it would have just been me, on my own, running in the cold morning darkness.

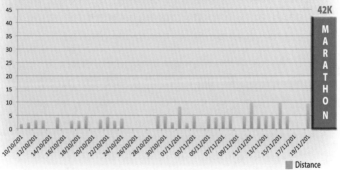

Week 6 Distance

Believe In What Is Possible

> *"What matters is not the idea a man holds, but the depth at which he holds it."*
>
> – EZRA POUND

I am a firm believer that the expectations we have – of our team, of other individuals, and of ourselves – have the most significant impact on the respective outcome. When we expect to fail, then we're already halfway defeated. Adopting a negative outlook is the first step on the road to failure. Think about it: how can you possibly provide your team with your alleged confidence in their ability to achieve difficult tasks if you yourself actually *expect* them to fail?

If you communicate that you expect your team to fail (and true intentions and feelings *will* become apparent at some point, no matter what), then it's as if you are communicating to them that *failure is permissible*. If it weren't, why would you give the team a task which you expect them to fail at?

When you give tasks to people whom you think will fail to accomplish them, then you are basically abdicating any accountability for success. If the team shows signs of failing, that result is simply meeting your expectations. Sadly, your response may be: *I told you so.* Even worse, you might not even feel obliged to step in or try to set things straight. This expectation, like all deeply entrenched expectations, becomes a self-fulfilling prophecy.

On the other hand, if you *do* expect a team to succeed, then you have set a completely different expectation! This is a whole other type of prophecy. You completely change the dynamics and you also take accountability for ensuring success. In a nutshell, your expectations directly impact how you communicate, interact, and manage the people around you. If you expect a team to succeed, you innately provide that team with your confidence in their ability – and the team feels this.

If you indeed believe that they can succeed, you should be able to articulate how. This is what gives the team the essential element of belief. Furthermore, if the progress doesn't meet your expectations along the way, then you will be much more inclined to step in. You will do your best to try and get the project back on track, and back in line with your expectations.

> *"High achievement always takes place in the framework of high expectation."*
>
> – CHARLES F. KETTERING

There have been a number of psychological experiments set up to test this hypothesis. Let's take a look at one such example: the 1968 Rosenthal-Jacobson Study. These experts showed that if teachers were led to expect an improved performance from some of the children in their classroom, then those particular children did indeed show improvement. The children were selected at random and their names were given to the teachers. As pupils, they were expected to achieve above-average improvements in their IQ. Over the course of the school year, these randomly selected children did indeed show these randomly predicted improvements.

What magic happened here?

No magic. It's just the incredible power of belief at work. Specifically, it's self-belief that's fuelled by the belief that others have in us. The way in which these teachers – based on their own expectations – interacted with and taught these children was what delivered the predicted improvements. The children felt the unquestionable confidence which the teachers had in them, and so fought to live up to those expectations.

Whilst many may doubt the power of positive expectations, I am sure that everyone will agree (and will have lived) with the consequences of negative expectations, i.e. when we set a self-fulfilling prophesy in motion. How many times have you envisioned failure, and then did not succeed – or, even worse, didn't even bother to try? But how many times have you envisioned success and felt really good about something, only to then sweep through it with flying colours? Think about it. Positive, great expectations cost you nothing. They set the right dynamics. They make everyone accountable for achieving success and therefore they increase the probability of success happening!

If you want your team to succeed, you need to set that expectation of success.

> *"Dream no small dreams, for they have no power to move the hearts of men."*
>
> – GOETHE

Marathon Diary

When I set out on my marathon journey, I realised the importance of belief. I have to believe that running a marathon is possible for me; if I don't, everything is just a farce. I need to visualise success. I need to see myself completing the training, getting fitter and faster. Finally, I need to visualise myself crossing the finishing line at the end of the marathon.

In other words, I have to eliminate all doubts.

The good news is I *have* eliminated them. I know that I am *not* too old, too unfit, or too busy. And I've been able to do so grounded upon my knowledge that these objections are weak. There are many people who are older or more unfit than I am who successfully run and compete in marathons.

As for the busyness factor, I've dealt with that too. Even back before I took up running, I was an early bird. I typically wake up at 6am, even though I don't leave for work until 8am. Usually I used to just drink tea, watch the news and read the papers. This means that I have at least one to one and a half hours per day that I now spend exercising, instead. Plus, I have the weekends. So 'I'm too busy' couldn't serve as an excuse either; that, too, got chucked out of the window.

I have a plan, I've found the time to train, and I truly believe that age and starting fitness and time are not limitations. I've got at least six months to prepare. The only things I have to master are commitment and determination. Given that (according to the people who know me) these are two of my defining characteristics, I'm not so worried.

With good progress being made, I am now running a 10K on a regular basis, and have also been able to extend my longest run to 13km. I'm feeling pretty good with my physical condition, and with the progress that I am making. More than ever, I believe that success is within my grasp.

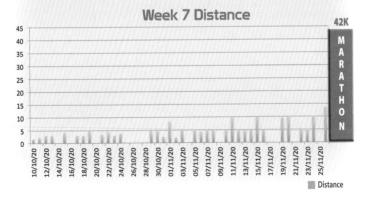

Week 7 Distance

Just Show Me How

> "If I had an hour to save the world, I would spend 59 minutes defining the problem and one minute finding solutions."
>
> – ALBERT EINSTEIN

More often than not, when teams fail to deliver or when they have poor results, it's usually because of a misguided focus. It isn't actually due to a lack of effort, commitment or desire. More often than not, it's simply due to a poor understanding of the problem or of the challenge that the team faces. They are zoning in on the wrong things.

So by all means, first define the problem.

If you don't know what the problem is, how can you solve it? How can you know if you do? Given the strict time pressures that we all experience at one point or another, the temptation to just tackle a solution before fully understanding the problem is commonplace and compounds the situation. But if leadership is about ensuring that we are all on the right track, then it is the leader who is accountable for fixing this problem.

Yup, that's you. You need to take a step back and confirm that the team is headed in the right direction. Or isn't.

At one company with which I was involved, the on-time delivery rate for projects was 26%. This meant that for every project requested by the business, the company had less than a one-in-three chance of the project being delivered on time. We experienced an average delay rate of *over three months.* And no, that wasn't something to cheer about.

Given that many of these projects were essential for business improvements or for the launch of new products, our delayed outcomes indicated really poor performance at our end. The first attempt to fix the problem was to encourage the developers to code faster; clearly, everyone assumed, it was the coders' fault that projects were not delivered on time. This had little to no effect, however. The delivery rate did increase incrementally, only up to 35%, which still meant that 65% of deliveries were late.

It was still tragic.

Our business partners were extremely frustrated with this performance. They could not schedule their own agendas accurately since they never knew whether they would receive their projects on time or not. Furthermore, there was a general bad vibe among the team. There was a feeling that we couldn't do any better, since this had been our level of performance for the last couple of years. We felt that we weren't up to anything more. We felt we couldn't succeed at more.

I stepped in to first define the problem, and *then* to come up with an effective solution. My belief is that every team can be successful if it focuses on what's important. Under my guidance, we carried out a detailed analysis of the entire beginning-to-end process to try and identify where the delays were being introduced. We captured as much data as possible, the start and end dates of each stage, the duration of each stage, and the key handover points between the various teams involved.

> *"All the so-called 'secrets of success'*
> *will not work unless you do."*
>
> – ANONYMOUS

As soon as we captured enough data, we continued our analysis in order to pinpoint the problems and identify potential solutions. As a result, we unearthed several patterns. This included the fact that many projects were late *before* we even began to build them!

It turns out that the build teams were unaware of the deadlines our company had committed to. Understandably, then, they were unaware that they weren't meeting the respective commitment. Since the deliveries were invariably late, the business partners were often unavailable to test them when they finally were delivered. This pushed the go-live dates back even further. Looking at the data, it was clear that pushing the developers for faster results was never going to be the solution, since slow development wasn't the problem. The issue was all about planning.

The main problem was that we'd been making commitments before we could grasp how long it was actually going to take us to deliver the product and before we could fathom what resources were available. Since the development teams were not involved in the overall project estimation process, they were delivering to dates that were important to *them* – but not to the business – and which weren't in line with the go-live date.

The lack of clear planning regarding the delivery time furthermore meant that we were scheduling unrealistic testing dates with the businesses. We also had some small issues regarding rework, where the development teams had not fully understood the requirements. Given all these issues, I would say that we were *lucky* to be delivering 26% on time...

And all this time, we had been unable to solve the issue because we had been focused on the wrong thing.

Clearly, we had some significant opportunities to improve performance. We took the bold step of explaining the situation to our business partners. To get their buy-in, we promised that – with some drastic changes in our process and with their support – we were committing to increase the on-time delivery of the enhancements to 80% within a six-month period.

> *"You cannot plough a field by turning it over in your mind."*
>
> – ANONYMOUS

In order to meet this goal of 80%, we revamped the whole end-to-end planning process:

✓ *The development teams sign off that they fully understand the requirements.*

✓ *They then create estimates on how long it will take to deliver the projects, but only when the blueprints have been signed off by our business partner.*

✓ *They reach an agreement with the business partner as to when they will be available to test the product, based on the new delivery date.*

✓ *The committed go-live date is decided, based on the above information.*

✓ *The go-live dates can only be changed by agreement with the business partner (provided that the change is due to the partner's unavailability).*

✓ *We implement these changes, and we continue to monitor and review the process. We also increase the management's attention, reviewing the data weekly to ensure that the changes are correctly implemented and lead to the performance improvements that we planned for.*

By the sixth month, we had increased the on-time delivery to a heartening 81%.

A beneficial side-effect of the whole process was that we'd also increased the communication between the businesses. This gave our partner businesses more control over the process. For instance, if one of the critical projects was going to be delayed, our partners were informed beforehand and could potentially work with the teams to re-plan priorities based on their own urgencies in order to ensure that their needs were met.

Initially when we tried to solve the on-time delivery rate, we focused on speeding up the development. Wrong priority; this didn't solve the problem. But we learned our lesson. Once you truly understand what the obstacle to your success was, only then can you tackle it. Once you see the hurdle, you can clear it. You are able to focus on your problems and transform poor performance into excellent performance in a short period of time.

"The measure of success is not whether you have a tough problem to deal with, but whether it is the same problem you had last year."

– JOHN FOSTER DULLES

Marathon Diary

We can all run to some extent, if our health permits it. But to run 26 miles is not something that many people actually do, especially if they don't have to. In fact, only 1% of the people on this planet have actually completed a marathon, though many more have failed trying. Prior to my personal commitment to this marathon, I would have said that the probability of me being able to complete such a race was *zero*. I would have said that 10K was my limit (and even then I would have had to train for weeks).

Now that I've publically committed, however, there is no going back.

So instead of thinking *why* I *can't* do it, why not focus on *how* I *can*? I've basically forced myself to change my mentality. Only thus can I be in the situation I am now: running, and determined to succeed.

Once I resolutely pushed myself into *solution mode*, I started to look at beginner marathon training plans, and I found one from Virgin. This plan lasts 26 weeks, starting very slowly with 15-20 minute daily runs during the first two weeks, if you remember, and building up: 30 minute runs by the end of Week 2, 40 minute runs by the end of Week 3, and so on. At Week 12, I'll be running half marathons. By Week 26, I should be ready to run my first marathon.

When I first looked at the plan I thought: *OK, breathe. The first two weeks are doable. I can definitely run for 15-30 minutes, and it doesn't seem to be much more than that until Week 4.* I knew that a 100-year-old man from India had completed a marathon, so I knew it was possible for me. Plus, I had a plan that I could believe in. I decided to try.

After a succession of 5km and 10km runs, I've run my first 15K! By now, I know *how* I can be successful. This confidence is like the winged sandals of Hermes on my feet. Now I just have to practise flying…

Week 8 Distance

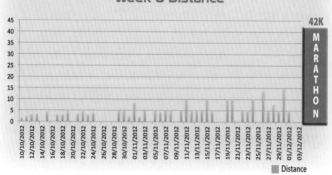

Eating the Elephant

> *"Footprints on the sands of time are not made by sitting down."*
>
> – THOMAS JEFFERSON

I am a huge fan of big, bold and aggressive goals. They're beautiful. And I do believe that goals need to be inspirational in nature, so they need to push boundaries; hence my love of audacious goals. However, there's a second part to this equation.

Once these goals have been set, then they need to be met.

You've likely heard the old adage: *If you're going to try eating an elephant, eat it one bite at a time.* I think it's fair to say that eating an elephant – metaphorically, of course, although I'm sure the same applies if you're going at it literally – is a big, audacious goal. Typically, we achieve such goals best if we learn to pace ourselves with a timeframe. If the target is big enough, then it shouldn't be against a frighteningly limiting deadline. We need to have a clear step-by-step approach which defines how we are going to achieve it if we do want to accomplish it. We need to apportion our time and energy wisely to ensure that we have the ultimate time and energy to reach the end.

The strategy is in creating those interim goals that will propel you forward so you can continue to achieve and proceed on a daily basis. You look ahead and focus on the ultimate goal, tackling one obstacle at a time. It's important to ensure that you are meeting it on schedule, so that you keep on track.

Remember to recognise and celebrate each interim goal that you complete. Know them for what they are: these are small successes on the road to the ultimate and grand victory. They are your stepping stones. Celebrating these, you'll see, will increase your motivation by providing you with a sense of accomplishment.

Keep the elephant in perspective. Know what you've done and what you still need to do, but savour each bite, and zone in on the next bite only when you've swallowed the previous one. Do keep the big goal there in the back of your mind, but *zone in* on the next 1% that you need to complete. If you complete 1% of the journey towards the target on a regular basis, then your success is all but guaranteed. All you need is time and determination.

Today and tomorrow and the day after that, don't focus on the whole two tons of elephant in front of you. There's no need to be daunted. Don't lose your confidence or your motivation. You can do it. Just focus on the next mouthful.

The mouth can only handle one mouthful at a time, anyway.

"Nobody trips over mountains. It is the small pebble that causes you to stumble. Pass all the pebbles in your path and you will find you have crossed the mountain."

– ANONYMOUS

When Alex Ferguson set his goal to knock Liverpool off their perch, he needed to win 13 League titles in order to achieve it. This certainly wasn't something that he could do in a single season – or in a single mouthful, so to speak. This was something that was going to take time.

Winning the title *once* would be a major achievement; in football, they often say that you need to focus on each game as it comes; if you look too far ahead, then you will lose focus, and consequently you'll get too far ahead of yourself and you'll slip and fall. This had been true of Alex Ferguson's predecessor, Ron Atkinson. By October, Manchester's team was 10 points ahead of its nearest rivals; Atkinson declared the championship to be 'a two-horse race' between Manchester and Liverpool.

But Atkinson had got too far ahead of himself, and as autumn transitioned to winter, his Manchester team began to falter. They ended up finishing *fourth,* behind Liverpool, Everton and West Ham. As a result, he was forever mocked by opposing fans who chanted "who came fourth in a two-horse race."

Ferguson knew better. He knew that to eat his elephant he needed to be patient. Also, he knew that he needed to make many fundamental changes to the club. Furthermore, he needed to ensure that the club had a solid financial basis in order to fund the purchase of the players he needed. Finally, he also knew that Manchester United needed their own talent development process in order to sustain the success that was essential for winning all 13 championships.

This goal was not something that could be done with a single team, or one star player. He would need to revamp the entire culture of the club. This is exactly what he accomplished, one season at a time, one game at a time, and one bite at a time.

Marathon Diary

For my goal of running a marathon, I had initially given myself a full 12 months to prepare so as to complete it successfully. Yes, this is still an aggressive goal for a non-runner who is way out of shape, but it isn't unreasonably aggressive.

A marathon is kind of a big deal, though. With my new plan and goal to run in Dusseldorf, I've now made that plan just a little more aggressive. Because when it comes to running a marathon, you can't just go out and do it. It's essential that you plan and prepare. Break down the timeline, the distances, and the intensity of the training. Take each session at point value; take them one at a time.

Remember that my first run was barely 15 minutes long. That's basically nothing when you consider that I will probably need to run *for five hours* in order to complete the full distance. Still, those 15 minutes were a start – a reasonable, bite-sized start – that I could do. It was progress.

Granted, it was difficult. In fact, it was the first time in at least a couple of years that I had run for 15 minutes straight. So you can imagine…

But if I had stopped to think about the marathon in its entirety, if I had beaten myself up by getting overwhelmed with the daunting prospect of *twenty-six entire miles*, I probably would have given up on the spot. I knew I had to strategise. Planning and focusing and following through, step-by-step, is the only way I'm going to eat my elephant: this marathon. I have to just focus on each run, completing each training session.

Nothing more, nothing less.

All I have to do is take it one day at a time. I constantly increase the time and distances that I run in order to build endurance. Each week, I run further and for longer. And my approach is now beginning to pay off. Having started with just a 15-minute jog, and increasing slowly but surely, Week 9 sees me passing another major milestone. I have managed to complete 21.1 kilometres! In other words, I've run my first-ever half marathon. It took two hours and 15 minutes.

If I accomplish this after just nine weeks, then completing a marathon after 26 weeks of training seems realistic. It just goes to show that, before you know it, you've eaten half the elephant!

Week 9 Distance

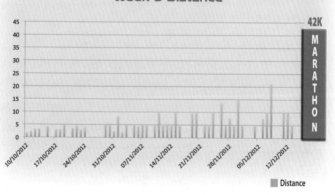

Happy Underachiever

> *"Action may not always bring happiness;*
> *but there is no happiness without action."*
>
> – BENJAMIN DISRAELI

When you're floundering, it may not be the strategic issues that are the problem.

Sometime the biggest challenge in improving an underachieving department is in actually getting the team to *realize* that their performance is actually not all that it could be...

In fact, your people might actually be quite happy with their performance and, while it might seem crazy to you, they're perfectly content. You could categorize them under a "happy underachiever" category. That's the point at which they're stuck.

And that's exactly what they are: stuck.

I'm sure you yourself are very aware of groups that fall into that category. Have you ever cheered for a sports team that—much to your own disappointment—were quite happy at finishing mid-table?

They had not challenged themselves to achieve their full potential; they were simply happy to be comfortably out of the relegation zone.

Whenever I raise the topic of "the happy underachiever", people tell me that it doesn't make sense.

"Surely that's an Oxymoron they say!" they say. *"How would anyone be happy with underachievement?"*

However, underachievers are often unaware of their situation. They either see their performance as adequate or they do not believe that they can do any better.

Therefore "improvement" isn't an option.

Sometimes, the first step is to simply awaken an underachiever to the knowledge of their potential. Often this is easier said than done. People don't like criticism, so even constructive criticism needs to be carefully managed. Therefore lead by example. Show them, be honest, and hold up that mirror so they can clearly see, for themselves, their underachievement.

You know that you have successfully accomplished this first step if the people on your team transform from happy underachievers to *unhappy* underachievers.

In the beginning, they may just be unhappy with you, because you have made them aware of their underachievement! No one wants to hear someone tell them they are not doing a good job. Remember messengers often get shot!

It is of paramount importance that you continue nourishing the productivity of your team. You want to encourage and inspire them, not just point out flaws. Never degrade them in any way! If you're not careful, the team can actually become permanently unhappy with *you*, rather than its own performance. Motivating and inspiring your team would be very difficult in those circumstances.

> *"Desire is the starting point of all achievement, not a hope, not a wish, but a keen pulsating desire which transcends everything."*

–NAPOLEON HILL

Unhappiness and inspiration are not good bed-fellows.

You need the team to harness their unhappiness and channel it into the development of their potential. It can become a very powerful source of energy and motivation, encouraging the team to embrace the changes that are necessary for success.

Take a moment to study the chart below, which shows the journey that a team, or any individual, makes on the path from being happy underachievers to becoming happy achievers.

Performance/Happiness Curve

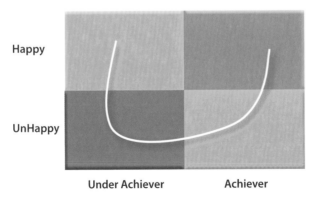

© Gordon Tredgold - www.Leadership-Principles

It is natural for the team to drop from happy underachieves to unhappy underachieves; it's a necessary part of the journey. Remember it is the team's unhappiness with their performance, along with your support and encouragement, which will drive them down the path to success.

Also remember that, as leaders, we need to use a great deal of tact and diplomacy in how we do this.

In reality, this amounts to *more encouragement* and *less criticism*. Talk more about how things can be done better, rather than focusing on what is being done poorly.

The chart's curve shows that even as people start to improve and achieve, they are still in the unhappiness zones for a while. This is where the use of rewards, and especially recognition, comes in. If people feel good about something that they're doing, they'll typically continue to do it. Remember the old adage: *what gets rewarded gets repeated.* As leaders our ultimate goal here is to convert happy underachievers into happy achievers.

Sometimes, an essential part of the solution for an under-performing team is the recruitment of a new leader. If the current leader has held his position for a number of years—without igniting improved results from his underachievers— that leader is probably part of the problem. The fresh perspective of a new leader can help make the necessary changes in the team.

I once worked with a company where I inadvertently made the team aware of their poor performance. I was then asked to manage them, which proved to be an interesting experience!

Their leader gave a presentation during which he claimed that his team had reduced costs by $20 million per annum. When it came to the Q&A Section, I asked where the rest of us could see the savings, which budgets had been reduced by the $20 million saved.

The room went pretty quiet.

No one had expected such a direct question, least of all the team leader, but I was simply asking to see where we could see the savings, to better understand how it had been achieved.

After a pause, the speaker tried to explain. He claimed that many of the savings were "estimated projected savings", based on cost avoidance. In other words the 'savings' would be created by not having to purchase additional hardware or higher more staff.

By the end of the presentation it was pretty clear to all of us in the audience that there were very few actual savings, and certainly nothing approaching the $20 million claimed earlier in the presentation. The team leader looked humiliated, which wasn't my intention, and later he told his team about my criticism of him and the team.

The team leader suggested that if *I* was so knowledge-able about cost savings, then maybe I should take over the project for the next year with the same goal of saving $20 million.

This wasn't a task I was keen to tackle. It wouldn't be easy under normal circumstances; but now, given that his entire team had gone from feeling like happy achievers to unhappy underachievers because of my comments during the presentation, it was going to be even more challenging.

As we started the project, I experienced a lot of resistance, and not surprisingly, the team's performance actually got worse. Fortunately, I had a couple of people on the team who were truly committed, and with whom I had worked before on prior projects.

I felt that it was important that our future saving should be independently verified and I agreed with the Finance Controlling Team that they would do this. I didn't want anyone in a meeting asking me to prove that our savings weren't just theoretical.

Given that the area we were looking at was the Data Centre, we knew that saving money would be a result of at least one of these three things:

✓ Reducing staff headcount;

✓ Reducing the amount of hardware; and/or,

✓ Reducing the amount of software.

Our initial focus was placed on hardware reduction. We had over 4,000 servers, and many of them cost hundreds of thousands of dollars per year. In fact, there were a couple of servers which cost us *over one million* a year! When it was first suggested that there might be over-capacity within the Data Centre, the team responded negatively. They said that they conducted yearly reviews and remained staunchly convinced that everything was operating efficiently. They were happy with their performance.

As a new leader, I asked for a review of server utilization, to better understand the situation. What we discovered was that there were a significant number of servers that had utilization of less than 1%. When challenged, it was said that these were back-up servers (in back-up mode, only utilised if the main server failed) and thus such minimal utilization was normal. This sounded like a reasonable answer, but what was interesting was that about 20% of all the servers seemed to be in this mode.

My two former colleagues on the team suggested we do a cross-check on that 20%, to see which systems those servers were attached to.

As a result, we found that 500 of these servers were not associated with any system at all! They were unused, just taking up space in the Data Centre and costing us far too much money, money that we didn't really need to spend!

This was a definite cost savings opportunity, which in turn saved us well over $7 million per annum.

It also showed the team that cost savings were possible, as long as we were open to looking at thing differently!

Shortly after this first breakthrough, I began to receive suggestions from the rest of the team. They brainstormed various ways by which we could save money, such as by transferring work between the servers and freeing up more servers so that we could shut those down too and stop paying for them. All of our savings were confirmed by the Finance Controlling Team, which really helped to create momentum. Bonuses were paid to the people who identified the biggest savings opportunities. By the end of the year, the entire team was fully engaged, with everyone seeking to squeeze out costs wherever possible.

Ultimately, we hit our savings target of $20 million and the team was at last extremely happy. This was a definite transition from happy underachievement to very happy achievement!

> *"Happiness lies in the joy of achievement and the thrill of creative effort."*
>
> – FRANKLIN D. ROOSEVELT

Marathon Diary

Before I started running, I'd always fooled myself into thinking that I was reasonably fit. I had previously lost a few kilos by dieting and exercising, and I played squash occasionally. At this point I would say that I was a happy average achiever—for my age, because everything is relative—rather than a happy underachiever.

However, my first training run was a real eye opener. It soon corrected that perception.

I only ran for 15 minutes at what I would now call a very modest pace. By the end I was so out of breath that you would have thought I'd just attempted to break the World 100 Meter Record.

To say that I wasn't *happy* with my fitness would be an understatement. I was seriously disappointed in myself; I had thought I was in much better shape than that. This first 'run' exposed me to the fact that I was definitely underachieving, and that I had significantly further to go than I'd initially thought.

I was now an unhappy underachiever. And this was good, because I now realised that there was no room for complacency in those early weeks of training, as I had so much more ground to make up than I first thought.

This week, having completed my first half marathon, running through the snow, three weeks ahead of schedule… it's probably fair to say that I am just a little bit pleased with myself ☺.

However, I won't consider myself a happy achiever until I cross the Marathon finishing line!

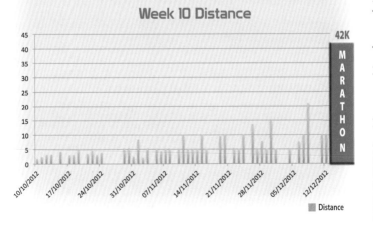

Week 10 Distance

MILE ELEVEN . . .

No Mañanas

*"Tomorrow is often the
busiest day of the week."*

– SPANISH PROVERB

We are all familiar with the term *procrastination.* It's the
process of putting things off until an indefinite 'later' for
any variety of reasons: we don't feel like doing whatever it
is that we have to do; we don't consider it important; we
hope it'll get solved on its own; we disillusion ourselves
that we're gaining 'free time' in the meanwhile, and so
forth. Regardless of the reason, the result is standard.

Procrastination is the first step we take down the road
to failure.

Who can ensure tomorrow? Who can ensure 'later'?
Something else might come up later. 'Later' might be a
bad time, an impossible time. Why put off something
that you can accomplish today? The cleanest and simplest
policy is to ensure that you make at least a bit of progress
every single day, as much as possible. Not only will you
be blessed with more peace of mind, but you'll get far
better results.

Take a minute and think back to that elephant we were chewing on. 'Do it today' doesn't always mean do it *all* today. Bite off what you can chew, then just chew it. If the project is projected to take 100 days of your time, look to make a minimum of 1% progress each and every day. If possible, try to get ahead of the schedule. Doing so will prove invaluable once you ease into the final stages, confident that you are well-positioned for success and that you're in control of the situation.

Think of it this way: leaving it all until the last minute is like finding yourself in a boxing ring, competing in a match where you're in desperate need of a knockout in the last round to win. Sure, you *might* get lucky, but why rely on scarce luck when you could have relied on your own powerful, intelligent self? Relying on luck is a strategy that can never *ensure* success. I've adopted the mantra *Hope is not a strategy!*

The solution? A '*no mañanas*' attitude. No tomorrows, no procrastination, and no delays – as far as possible. Instil this mentality into your team, and watch as productivity soars.

More often than not, we *do* start out with good intentions. You might tackle a project today – with great gusto and enthusiasm, even – but often the project gets bogged down in the planning or in the endless discussions concerning the requirements. You try to get everything perfectly aligned before you start actual development. Or you lose your motivation or enthusiasm when something knocks the wind out of your sails.

Too many times, I have seen projects where the budget has been split like so: over 50% of the cost goes to analysis and design, 30% on development, and a mere 20% is dedicated to testing and implementation. Invariably, these are the projects that fail (and badly) with costly overruns. Typically, this is because the project team has procrastinated during the analysis phase, suffering from the illusion that they have more than enough time… only to discover later that the project is awfully behind schedule.

> *"Nothing is so fatiguing as the eternal hanging on of an uncompleted task."*
>
> – WILLIAM JAMES

We often plan projects with the optimistic outlook that everything will proceed beautifully. That's not a bad mentality to have – in fact, nothing great was ever achieved without enthusiasm, according to Ralph Waldo Emerson. The danger is in leaving this outlook in the realm of theory; if you don't want it to rot, you've got to plant it into your life and tend to it. You have to *do*, and not just *assume*.

If you plan tasks according to their deadlines, there's your red flag. If you need to install hardware, and you know that the process takes two weeks, you should give yourself three weeks of breathing room. Murphy's Law states that problems will crop up when you most desperately need things to run smoothly, so plan wisely and give yourself room to adjust. If a task is not dependent on the completion of a previous task, why not start it at the earliest possible moment? Be kind and give yourself that breathing room.

I remember working on a billing project for a major utilities company. I'm talking about a twelve-month project with a fixed deadline due to changes in government legislation. The project was extreme, requiring changes in many processes; we moved from a regulated utilities system to a deregulated system, where different regions could compete for customers across the United Kingdom. Happily, the software delivery was completed just in time.

Unfortunately, the project still failed to go live on time.

Can you guess where we slipped? We needed new stationery for the invoices, and there was a lead time of four weeks in order to get that stationery. Scheduling around the completion deadline, the business postponed ordering the stationery until exactly four weeks prior to the go-live date. However, due to the Easter holiday, the printers couldn't guarantee on-time delivery...

This meant that despite the fact that we'd developed the complex system, changed the business process, and trained the end users, the project couldn't go live simply because we hadn't ordered the *stationery* in time! The stationery element was probably the least complex component, but nevertheless it caused a terrible amount of inconvenience and trouble. Because we'd left it for the eleventh hour, the delay due to the delivery issue drastically impacted the entire project.

> *"Saints are sinners who keep on going."*
>
> – ROBERT LOUIS STEVENSON

Marathon Diary

This week I've been on holiday in Australia, so I'm completing the runs along Melbourne's St. Kilda beach. It is absolutely stunning. I've done a mix of 5km and 10km runs. I'm taking care to not overdo it since the temperature here is between 15-25C (quite a difference from the very chilly Dusseldorf!).

I'm feeling good because I'm on schedule. If I wasn't, I'd be freaking out. When I committed to the marathon, I spent the first few days looking for a training plan. I found my 26-week plan; given that the Dusseldorf Marathon was 30 weeks away, I was delighted, believing that I could complete the training and still have four entire weeks to spare.

I cheered inside my head. *OK! I will go out this weekend and get myself some training kit and some new running shoes. I'll start the following week, and that'll be my Week One!*

The following morning I woke up at 6am as usual. I sat down and switched on the TV to watch the early morning news, and I suddenly thought to myself: *Why am I not running now?* The kit was just an excuse. I had enough kit to run for 15 minutes. I didn't need state-of-the-art Nike running gear or new shoes for that! I saw what I was doing for what it was: a delaying tactic. So I decided to give myself a taste of my own medicine.

No mañanas. Start right now.

I went and changed my clothes, and by 6.15am I'd hit the pavement. I know that if I had waited a week, I probably would have found another reason to stall. If I did that, then my training programme would be too tight. I already understood that there would be days when I wouldn't be able to run, due to really bad weather or even an injury; if too many of those piled up, I wouldn't be able to complete the training prior to the marathon. That meant that I would have to wait for the next marathon!

I want to run *this* one.

Realising all that, I'd made my decision. I put a stake in the ground and just started. Some people later asked me: "Why 6am? Why out of the door by 6.15?" Why not give myself time to 'wake up' and get some coffee or tea into my system first?

I give the same answer that I give to myself every day: *If I wait another hour to run today, that's an extra hour to come up with a really good reason why I shouldn't run.* We're all masterminds at coming up with reasons like that. It's good to exercise in the morning, before your brain really figures out what you're up to. If I am running before I am fully awake, it's too late for me to bail out; I'm already running when I manage to come up with the reasons for not running! And I'm not stopping then.

Something else that really helps with this is the accountability factor. The companionship of running with a couple of friends is priceless. We all know that we cannot go back in time, and every missed session reduces our preparation. With insufficient preparation, we reduce our probability of success. We all know how important the training regime is, so we push each other to keep running and to not miss a training run. Peer pressure at its finest!

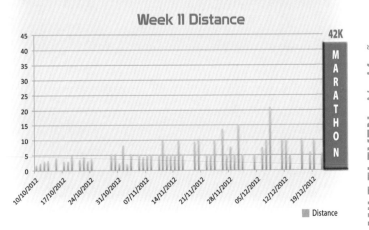

Week 11 Distance

MILE ELEVEN - *No Mañanas*

Attitude vs. Aptitude

*"I may not be there yet, but I'm closer
than I was yesterday."*

– ANONYMOUS

Aptitude is about having the ability, talent or competency to perform a particular task or job. When recruiting, employers often focus on aptitude; they look for people with the best skills for the job, and then they tend to choose the most highly qualified person. When assessing people in annual reviews, there is often a focus on ability (technical or managerial) and on potential, as well as on performance.

However, if there is one thing I have learned after years of delivering large complex change programmes, it is that it's actually *attitude*, in fact, which drives things to completion. Attitude is all about belief, mindset and the determination to do a job. It is determination, that *never-say-die* attitude, which guides us to overcome complex technical problems that more 'experienced' professionals struggle to solve.

You can see this pattern in the sports world, too. It's not always the most talented player who wins. In fact, it's often the most determined person, the player with the most heart, the guy or girl with the most commitment – that's the person who overcomes the more talented opponent.

Knowing this, when I look to recruit staff now, my primary focus is on attitude, not aptitude.

If I have someone with the right attitude, I can always work to provide them with the aptitude to do the job; the skill-set is just that: a skill, and one that can be learned. On the other side of the spectrum, things get messier. It's much harder to instil in someone the right attitude, no matter how much expertise that person carries.

If genius is indeed 1% inspiration and 99% perspiration, that attests to 1% aptitude and 99% attitude! Imagine how hard it is to force the 99% of perspiration, having only 1% of the equation on your side. If you have someone with the right attitude, however, you've ensured the 99% per-spiration, at which point you're only looking to ignite that 1% inspiration in order to achieve the stroke of genius, or success.

The ideal? Enlisting someone with the right attitude *and* the right aptitude. But it's not always an ideal world, so in the face of decision-making, I'll take attitude every time.

When it comes to leadership, I think this differentiation is even more significant. Leaders set the culture for their organisation. They instil the tone, the mood and the mindset of the people they lead and serve. A lack of good attitude in a leader inevitably fosters a lack of good attitude within the entire organisation. If you want your organisation to be successful, pick a leader with the right attitude, and he or she will set the tone and pace within the entire organisation.

> *"The difference between try and triumph is a little umph."*
>
> – ANONYMOUS

Marathon Diary

This week finds me in Cairns, Northern Queensland, running through high humidity at a steady 32C. The terrain is very hilly, which is excellent for strength training; I've been running mostly 5Ks but I managed to squeeze in a 12km run as well.

Back home, I normally start running between 5.30 and 6am. If the weather's not too bad, there are usually one or two other runners about. If it's good, we usually see quite a few more (maybe as many as 10 to 15). If there is snow or rain, though, it might just be me and my team – Tarak, Dave and me. Some weekends when they aren't available, I'm the only one.

This doesn't deter me anymore; on the contrary, it motivates me. I know my preparation is not being impacted because I'm not stopping, and this will give me an advantage as soon as the weather picks up since I'm the one who's faithfully on schedule. Because, honestly, I don't have the aptitude for being a great runner. I'm not the best runner out there, not by a long shot. It seemed I was always slower than everyone else. However, I have a far more powerful weapon.

Determination.

I have attitude. I have a great competitive edge. I hate to get knocked down by anything. My satisfaction emerges from achieving the goals that I set for myself. This is why I knew that when I committed, especially publicly, to running a marathon, I would do it. It works in my favour, of course, that this is not a race based on speed. It's about endurance and determination, so it brings out the best in me, for I'm nothing if not determined. I am committed and have put my body on the line to run 26 miles.

Without the right attitude, how can I ever succeed? Even if I have all the credentials and abilities to run and finish the race in *first place*, I'll fail as miserably as the Hare in Aesop's fable if I lack the attitude to keep up till the end.

My training began in October 2012. My 26-week training plan meant that I would need to train during the winter months in order to be ready for the marathon on 28 April 2013. It's not aptitude that gets me out of bed to run at 6am most mornings. It's not what makes me run when it's raining, snowing, or sub-zero degrees outside.

That's *all* about attitude.

This was the weather when I ran my first half marathon. It was cold (-3C), as you can fathom from the photograph; two inches of snow and sub-zero temperatures are not going to stop me. I was determined to do it. I also know that if I can run half a marathon in these conditions, I will definitely be able to complete a full marathon in April weather. Of course, other folks might be training on a treadmill in a gym, but it's not the same as running on the road. Who's to know what the weather will be like in April, anyway? Snows are not unheard of. If it does snow, then I will be prepared! Even if we get a heat wave, I've run in temperatures reaching 32C with very high humidity, up there in the rainforests and hilly terrain of Cairns.

I might not be the fittest or the fastest, but there will be few competitors who will be more determined than me.

In a battle between man and the weather, this time *man won*!

Week 12 Distance

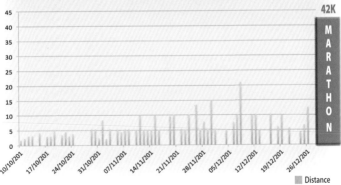

Distance

What Got You Here Won't Get You There!

> *"There is no education like adversity."*
>
> – DISRAELI

Grab the rungs and start to climb up the professional ladder, and you'll discover that the key to advancement is flexibility. The skills and expertise that get you one foot or 100 feet off the ground will not be enough to brave the winds once you get to the next rung. As a result, you might find that you're suddenly out of your depth at those higher levels when different skills are required (e.g. management and leadership skills).

A lot of this is explained in the Peter Principle, a theory which states: *In a hierarchy, every employee tends to rise [up] to his level of incompetence.*

It makes sense when you pause to think about it. You do a job well, you're promoted; you do the next job well, you're promoted again. This happens in succession until you eventually rise to a position where your plate is full or your skills can't buoy you up further. When you can no longer perform at an optimal level, you've reached the ceiling between your competence and incompetence; your 'level of incompetence', if you prefer.

This happens when the skills required of you for your new role are different from those which allowed you to be successful up to this point. Sometimes, you can learn and attain the new expertise; however, until you do so, you lack the training or the competence required. You realise that in order to survive in the new territory, you need to adapt.

Right now, you're probably an expert at something. It could be risk management, it could be car mechanics, it could be snowboarding, it could be cooking *pasta alla carbonara*. Being an expert means that you've acquired enough know-how which enables you to excel yet which also enables you to help others (i.e. your team), given your specific knowledge. You are able to use your technical expertise to guide other experts, while you're simultaneously able to continue with the hands-on work yourself. A subtle transition into a low position of leadership is usually easy, as you still have the opportunity to monitor and correct mistakes through your own efforts. At that point, you can still be a leader who 'manages'.

Once you are promoted to new heights – as when you become responsible for multiple teams – then there's much more required of you. Suddenly, you need different skills. You discover that your technical expertise becomes less valuable and your management skills become much more important. Now you need to focus on planning, control systems, feedback mechanisms, performance reviews, salary reviews, staff development, and so forth. As you advance even further to managing departments, regions, or even global organisations, you realise that you won't be able to hold on to this rung if you can't master these new skills.

The higher you climb, the harder you could fall. It's suicidal to go bungee-jumping without a tried-and-tested rope. If you don the mantle of your organisation's visionary and motivational coach, which is a far cry from what you had to do at the start of your career, you had best be prepared. Are you? It's likely that you have not been taught these specialised skills during your earlier technical role, so you must be adaptable and open to learning these new skills later.

It's also true that some skills may conflict and might not help you advance. Just because someone is the best football player on the field doesn't mean that he would make the best manager. It's not *impossible*, but statistically it's been shown that all the best football managers were not the best footballers.

> *"It is not the strongest of the species that survives, nor the most intelligent, but the one most responsive to change."*
>
> – ANONYMOUS

As you progress, you need to be able to learn new and essential skills. Perhaps you'll be provided with training, but such skills are not easily learned in the classroom. What's worse, you may be trained by the wrong person and thus misguided. Taken under the wing of a mentor, you may discover that you've been paired with someone who has progressed without the right skills for her current role, and consequently she compounds the problem; a case of the blind leading the blind, so to speak.

I remember my first day as Project Manager in a certain company. Prior to that, I had been Functional Architect, Test and Implementation Manager for a certain system of which I had now become Project Manager. It was familiar territory, so I thought it'd be a piece of cake. No one knew the system better than I did, after all; I had designed it, tested it, and implemented it. So theoretically, I knew everything. Right?

In reality, however, all that knowledge and expertise was useful for no more than 10% of my new responsibilities.

What had got me 'here' was not enough to get me 'there'. On my first day at this new post, I was requested to meet with my Test Manager. She was clearly upset about something, and explained that she needed my help. Piece of cake, right? I could solve anything around here! After all, I was a not only a testing expert; I had designed the entire testing suite for this system. What could she throw at me that I could not fix?

When I sat down in the meeting she dropped the bomb.

"I have found a lump in my breast and I am scared that it's cancer," she told me. "What should I do?"

Nothing in my career had prepared me for that moment. All of a sudden, it hit me that *leading* was very different from *doing* (or even *managing*, for that matter). Dealing with such situations was not in the manual. It had not been covered on any of the project management or leadership trainings that I had taken.

I managed the situation in the only way I knew how: by showing I cared and trying to console her. I did my best to ensure that she sought medical attention. As it turned out, thank goodness, it was just a lump, not cancer. For me, however, it was an immense lesson, illuminating that I still had an awful lot to learn.

I was fortunate that since I was very well-versed regarding the system itself, the actual work related to the system only demanded a small amount of my time. Thus, I could devote most of my time and energy to things not directly related to the system: managing the *people*. Since only 10% of my prior expertise was valuable to me now, I had to learn the other 90% about the job rapidly, on the job, as quickly and as effectively as possible.

My boss, like many bosses, had just assumed that since I had been good at what I had done before, I would work to be just as great in my new role. Unfortunately, many bosses make such assumptions. But the fact was I wasn't properly prepared for this role!

As you boost people up to positions of senior management and leadership, you need to ensure that you provide them with the skills they need in order to succeed at what they need to do. It's your job and responsibility to share the keys for success. Otherwise, you are looking for trouble; you will have implemented the Peter Principle, promoting people to a level where they will be incompetent and may fall flat on their faces.

First and foremost, you need to ensure that you yourself are on the right track. If you reach a level where you find yourself overwhelmed, overestimated or overcome, you need to take a step back and go back to the drawing board. You need to reassess yourself and your strategy. Minds, like nappies, need constant changing. Your decisions are only as sound as the information on which you base them.

Human existence is based on *evolution.* If we don't evolve, we won't progress. And if we can't progress, we can't succeed.

> *"When you are through changing, you are through."*
>
> – BRUCE BARTON

Marathon Diary

This week I completed my second half marathon, finishing precisely at 1:59:58. Exactly *just* under two hours! I can't believe I have at last broken this personal barrier. Have you ever looked back and found yourself astonished (in a good way!) with your own victory and progress? Ah, it's a spectacular feeling!

When I shared the news with some of my fellow runners, they also couldn't believe the progress I've made. One of them even commented that, given this rate of progress, not only will I finish the marathon, but I will also do it in less than four hours! He predicted that I will complete it in 3:45, which would exceed all of my expectations.

As a Christmas present, instead of buying running gear or any such material gift, Dave bought me a couple of training sessions with a running coach. I was ready to gear up with some excellent expert advice concerning nutrition, running poise and style, and more. Yes, I can appreciate anything that'll give me a bit more advantage and training!

When Dave and I first met Adam, our coach, I was surprised to discover that he was pretty concerned about us. He thought that we were running too fast. He called us *marathon virgins*. We should focus on running slower, he advised, because we had to learn to conserve our energy.
42 kilometres wasn't a mere hop and a skip. It was a long way.

I proudly replied that I had just run a half marathon in under two hours, and still had half my training to go.

"So what?" Adam shrugged. "A half marathon is not a full marathon. You can complete a half marathon without drinking, without eating. The human body can operate for two hours with little or no problem, no need for nutrition or refuelling. This is not the case for a full marathon." He asked us whether we were running in fat-burning or carb-(sugar) burning mode.

"I don't know," I said. "How can we tell? What's the difference?"

Turns out we really needed a coach.

Adam explained to us that the human body has approximately 5,000 calories of energy stored up in the body as sugar – and up to 160,000 calories stored as fat! The calories of sugar are the easiest to use, but they'll only keep you going for about two hours. After that, you need to refuel. That's why most people hit the wall after two hours when they're competing in marathons. Around that two-hour point, most of them are suddenly plagued by cramps and muscle fatigue, caused by the lactic acid that is created because of the sugar-burning through anaerobic exercise.

I was dumbfounded. All this time, I'd thought I'd been on the right track! In a mere 13 weeks I'd transformed myself from a sedentary non-runner to a fit 52-year-old runner who had completed two half marathons (one in less than a two-hour timeframe!). But suddenly I wasn't sure if I had what it took to keep going until the very end.

Adam scheduled me for an aerobic test to see at what speed my body switched from burning fat to burning sugar. The results are outlined in the graph below. The green line shows the amount of fat I am burning; the axis shows the speed at which I am running. The important point is the one at which the green line crosses the axis. For me, this point was 6.5km per hour, which equates to a fast walk.

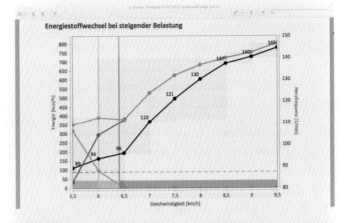

Energiestoffwechsel bei steigender Belastung

"What does that mean?" I asked Adam.

"As you start to run," he explained, "you are burning sugar. The training you have done is wonderful for a half marathon, but will not get you through a full marathon. I'm afraid that you will run out of energy and your body will start to shut down. You can try and eat to refuel along the way, but since your digestive system will be shutting down, even that may not work."

Bad news. All of the training I have done up to now is ideal for a half marathon, but not good enough for a full marathon. What had got me here will not see me get over the finish line.

Adam didn't leave us without hope, however. He says it is possible for us to adapt the training, and in the 13 weeks remaining we can prepare properly in order to complete the marathon successfully. This

MILE THIRTEEN - *What Got You Here Won't Get You There!*

101

will involve running at a much slower pace, at around 6-7km an hour, and running with a heart rate that is just 60-70% of our maximum. Over time, we can increase speed while keeping our heart rates steady. Doing this will enable us to run faster and burn *fat*, not sugar.

It is disheartening to learn that we'll have to completely revamp our process; at the same time, it is also motivating to learn that we have a new strategy that helps us turn the situation around. Ultimately, running in a fat-burning mode will be healthier for us. We'll experience a lot less fatigue and fewer cramps, and – most importantly – it will keep us from 'hitting the wall', or at least reduce its impact.

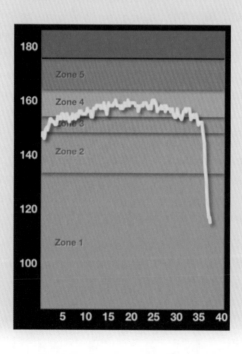

The chart on the left shows heart rate during the running: when the heart rate is in the green zone, then I am burning fat and I'm in the right mode to run the whole length of the marathon. Whenever the heart rate is in the yellow, amber or red zones, I am doing it wrong. I need to train my body to be able to run at a lower heart rate for longer.

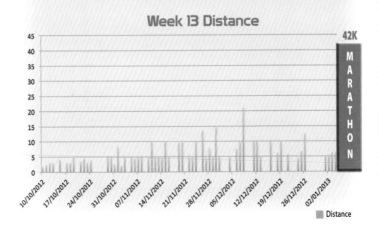

Week 13 Distance

MILE THIRTEEN – *What Got You Here Won't Get You There!*

MILE FOURTEEN...

Measuring for Success

> *"Strategy without tactics is the slowest route to victory. Tactics without strategy is the noise before defeat."*
>
> – SUN TZU

There's an old saying that is golden in its wisdom: *What you measure, you improve.* That is something I strongly believe in, but the half of the wisdom of that saying is in its implication. It's important that you know *what* to measure. You need to measure the right things. Measurement:

- ✓ *Provides a baseline of performance against which we can show improvement.*
- ✓ *Communicates what we see as important and can provide focus.*
- ✓ *Provides important data which can be analyzed to identify improvements.*
- ✓ *Offers a basis for target setting, bonus schemes, reward and recognition.*

My first conscious experience with measurement happened when I was a young man and an enthusiastic rugby team member. At one point, I remember how the team enlisted a new coach. This guy was a very passionate advocate of measurements and metrics. He called them 'the tools to improve our winning record'.

When he joined our team, we were winning approximately 50% of our games. Although we scored lots of points during our games, we also conceded a bunch of points. The coach decided that our defence needed improvement. Under his guidance, then, we started to count the number of tackles made by each player and we compared those to our expectations. This helped us identify the players who were not involved enough in defence. Inevitably, the number of tackles increased.

We didn't see any tangible improvement, however, because we still conceded too many points. Since points were scored when tackles were missed, rather than when tackles were made, our coach began instead to count the number of tackles *missed* by each player.

After reviewing this information, what we realised was that the players who were making high numbers of tackles were the ones who were also missing the most tackles. This meant that we were focusing on the wrong area. We had been improving the tackle counts of players who had low tackle counts to begin with, but we had not been addressing the missed tackles, where we were conceding points.

> *"Opportunities do not come with their values stamped upon them."*
>
> – MALTBIE BABCOCK

The coach increased our training in tackling. While this did lead to some improvements in technique, it didn't significantly reduce the number of missed tackles. Our overall performance still did not improve. So, to gain more insight, the coach looked to identify *when* the tackles were missed. We noted that several players, especially those heavily involved in defence, would miss very few tackles during the majority of the game, but they often started to lag during the last 10 minutes.

At last it became clear that the issue wasn't tackling technique. It was timing. It was fatigue. It was our level of fitness.

He worked to improve our fitness training, focusing on stamina as well as power and speed. He also arranged to substitute some players during the last 10-15 minutes, replacing them with fresher players. Finally, we started to see improved results. We still scored as many points as before, but the number of conceded points had drastically reduced. Consequently, our winning percentage increased!

The coach's strategy took time, it evolved, and it guided us slowly but steadily to success. By learning how to measure and assess measurements, we had defined the problem and ultimately solved it.

I learned from this that it's true that you measure what you improve, but it's equally as important to ensure that you measure the correct things if you want to achieve precise results. You need to constantly review the process and ensure that you are working towards what you want and need. Even if things seem hopeless, don't give up. It's usually the third or fourth iteration of the measurement process that identifies the real problem. Don't spend too much time perfecting the first set of measurements. If it's not working, tweak your tactics. Be flexible and diligent until you flesh out the strategy that will ensure your success.

> *"A wise man will make more opportunities than he finds."*
>
> – FRANCIS BACON

Marathon Diary

Hey, I'm only human. I enjoyed the Christmas and New Year holidays, the dinners were to die for, and my running was impacted a little. On average, though, I did manage to run every other day.

Having been told that I'm running too fast and that I need to improve my performance at the lower heart rate, I've bought a heart rate monitor. I want to ensure I am measuring the right thing before I focus on successfully completing the marathon. My heart rate should stay in the green zone. This requires me to run more slowly, which also builds up endurance. In order to run faster, you need to build endurance, and you build endurance by running slower. As counter-intuitive as it may seem, it works.

The graph below demonstrates a run during which my heart was pumping almost always in the green zone. When I ran at this pace, I noticed that the stiffness in my legs was significantly lessened, even though I had slowed the pace marginally. It makes me wonder if I could actually finish the marathon with a smile and without limping around the house for a week afterwards!

I have now re-set my goal: complete the marathon; raise some money; and finish healthy, in one piece, and with a smile. I'm also thinking how wonderful it would be simply to enjoy the whole event!

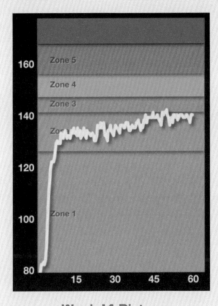

Week 14 Distance

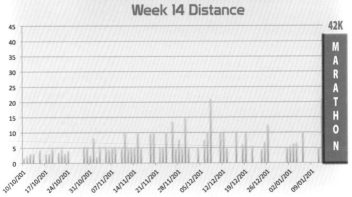

Distance

MILE FIFTEEN . . .

Effective vs. Efficient

> "God gave us two ends - one to sit on
> and one to think with.
> Success depends on which one you use.
> Head you win, tail you lose."
>
> – ANONYMOUS

There is a big difference between being efficient and being effective. When you're committed solely to efficiency, you want the quickest and easiest solution – *now.* Your tap erupts and you need to fix it before the house floods, so you sprint to the garage, grab two bucket-loads of tools, and try every single hammer, screwdriver and wrench that you've got.

Are you efficient? Absolutely; you haven't even stopped to wipe the sweat off your face. But are you effective? Sounds like you're not much of a plumber, because the water is still spraying everywhere. So no, I wouldn't exactly call you effective.

Now say that the tap breaks and, this time, you pause to brainstorm the best strategy. Sure, you could panic or consider yourself an amateur professional, and you may be drilling and cutting and wrenching for 10 hours straight – and you might even fix the problem. But a far more effec-

111

tive option would be to turn off the water, whip out your phonebook, and call your local plumber. The plumber will come with his tool kit, he'll know exactly what to do, and he'll fix it. If he's not your brother, chances are that he'll charge you for the job, but in a matter of minutes your kitchen will probably be habitable again. That sounds pretty darn effective to me.

When we are efficient, it means that we complete our tasks with the minimum amount of time or effort. Efficient screams: *Get someone in here right away!* Effective urges: *Make sure you get the right person in here.* Mr. Effective knows that if we are not focused on the right things, Mr. Efficient is actually no more than wasted time and wasted effort. Many companies, however, seem to favour Mr. Efficient. We often forget that in order to be effective, we need to ensure that we have the correct focus first. If you do the wrong job, it doesn't matter how well you do it or how good you are at it; it will not lead you to your desired results.

The fact is you will make more progress towards your goal if you do the right job poorly than if you do the wrong job brilliantly. As a leader, it is your job to ensure that your organisation is focused on the right tasks; as a manager, it's your job to ensure that these tasks are done well. It's a matter of blending both effectiveness and efficiency.

Focus is extremely important. Misaligned focus is not just a matter of wasted time and effort; it can easily become a matter of unhealthy morale and diminished motivation. You need to see *results*: that's your deserved reward for working hard, after all. With the wrong focus and the wrong results, your team might never achieve their goals. If you don't know that the focus is wrong, you might wrongly assume that it's the 'quality of work' that is stopping you from being effective. You then focus on working harder (on improving efficiency), yet it's all in vain. Free yourself from this downward spiral, which will continue to frustrate and demotivate you, by reassessing the effectiveness of your labours.

Once you know what your objective is and once you can clearly articulate it, you must evaluate everything you do and determine whether it helps you in achieving that objective. If it doesn't help, stop doing it; it's wasted performance. Your drive for efficiency has to be combined with a drive to ensure that you are focused on the right job. High-performing teams are not necessarily the ones who do outstanding work. High performance is achieved by doing the *right* job and doing it *well*.

In order to be effective, you need to have a clear idea of what success looks like and to know what is needed in order to accomplish it. Once you have oriented yourself with this knowledge, you can be confident that you've tackled the right job and that you're focusing correctly. And only then, at last, will you begin to make progress. That is the goal: to be effective, *to deliver the intended result successfully.*

> *"We are too busy mopping the floor to turn off the faucet."*
> –ANONYMOUS

For an example close to home, check out your neighbourhood's football field. People assume that the team which possesses the ball for the longest period during the game is the one that wins the most games. While this statistic is true, what is even truer is that 100% of teams that score the most goals win 100% of those respective games. If your focus is just on creating a high possession percentage but you don't score any goals, how can you win the game? You won't. If you've got 100% of possession of the ball in your own half of the pitch, you're amazing at efficiency... but you haven't been very effective. That's not the formula for winning the game.

What's the goal? The goal is to win the game, yes? So your focus has to be on *scoring more goals than the opposition*. It's that simple. Sure, you may use a high possession percentage to ensure that your opponent has fewer opportunities to score, but your game plan must also include creating good quality opportunities for your own team to kick and score. Be effective by identifying the right things to focus on, and then work to become more efficient in doing them.

Having defined *effectiveness*, the team will immediately begin to see progress as they focus. After that, it's just a matter of time and perseverance. Results appear, motivation flourishes, morale improves, and the job is successfully accomplished. The better the results, the greater the motivation. The cycle feeds itself. That is the positive, upward-aimed spiral towards success. That is the way to create a high-performance culture and a high-performing team.

In my first job, I was the production manager in a textile factory, where we produced different products with different colour patterns and different thread patterns (10 threads, 12 threads, 14 threads, 16 threads, and 18 threads per inch). We had five machines, and each time we had to change one product with a certain thread pattern to another pattern (say from 10 threads to 12 threads), that machine was unproductive for up to four hours.

The previous manager realised how important it was to reduce this downtime. He tried to train the teams in reducing the time that it took for them to switch from product to product. This strategy bought them an hour of time; he eventually reduced the five-hour-long downtime to the current four hours, which was a sizeable 20% improvement.

When I joined, the teams were still trying to find ways to reduce the lost time. As a new member, I had little experience. However, I also didn't understand why things were done the way they were; I asked a lot of questions. When I watched the teams working hard to reduce the time for the change of pattern, I asked why we even had to change thread patterns in the first place.

"What do you mean?" they asked.

For me, it seemed simple. We had five machines and five different thread patterns. Why not have just one setting per machine? Then we wouldn't need to waste four hours while waiting for a pattern switch. A colour change only needed two hours, not four.

My question ("how can we reduce the number of pattern changes?") revealed that the team had been asking the wrong question all along ("how can we make the pattern change faster?"). They had been focusing on how they could be more efficient at what they were doing, instead of focusing on a new way to change what they were doing to be more effective.

Given just this simple change, we were able to increase productivity by 50% without changing anything else.

> *"You must not only aim right, but draw the bow with all your might."*
>
> – HENRY DAVID THOREAU

Marathon Diary

In the running world, the difference between *efficient* and *effective* is more than a spelling issue. *Effective* means keeping the goal in mind: for me, that's to complete the marathon. If I wanted to focus on efficiency, I'd probably be trying to run as fast as possible now – say 15km/hour – but there's no use in that if I can't complete a 42km distance at that pace. To be effective, I needed to be able to complete the full distance.

It helps to remind myself that am the Tortoise, not the Hare. Speed is not my forte, so prizing speed over completion equates to failure. Speed does play a

LEADERSHIP - *It's a Marathon not a Sprint*

role, of course. With a time limit of five hours and 30 minutes, I'll need to be able to complete 10km in an average of 75 minutes in order to finish the marathon effectively. It is possible to run more efficiently and for longer, but the point is to complete the distance in the allotted time. If I haven't covered a distance of 10km in 75 minutes, then, in all likelihood, I will fail to complete the marathon on time.

Knowing this allows me to calculate an effective running pace where I need to run 1km within an average of seven and a half minutes. If I'm slower, I'll run out of time. If I'm faster, I'll possibly run out of steam.

Great progress this week, ran two half marathons in a week. Looking good and feeling confident. Dave and Tarak ran their first half marathons, so this was a major milestone for both of them.

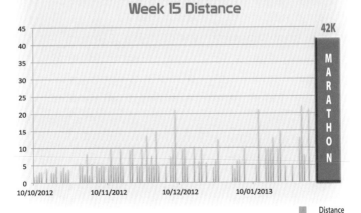

Week 15 Distance

The Art of Motivating

> *"Whatever the mind of man can conceive and believe, it can achieve."*
>
> – NAPOLEON HILL

Your words can be your most powerful weapon, your most effective tool, and your most treacherous messenger. The tongue can be a double-edged sword. It can heal or it can harm. In the business world, as in any other aspect of life, your words and your behaviour have a critical impact on your dealings and interactions with other people. Has anyone ever given you blended feedback? Anything like: "You know, that was a great job, *but it's a shame about the cost overrun.*" Or something like: "Fantastic design concept... *but it's a shame about the colour.*"

Stop to think about what such phrases are actually doing.

What is their purpose? Is the speaker really seeking to motivate someone, or to admonish them? Does he want to praise, or punish? Most likely, he is trying to do both at once, which is why both concepts are vying for attention in the same sentence! But people can't accept an equal dose of praise and punishment so simply. Innately, we humans allow negativity to weigh down on us more heavily than positivity. We are constantly on the alert for negative messages, rejecting messages, and hurtful messages. The more we hear them, the more defensive and resentful we may become.

When it comes to encouraging and motivating others, it's critical that you focus only on positive messages. That's not to say you can never criticise or punish someone for something he's done wrong; if you don't point out the mistakes, that person might never learn or grow. But the key is not to taint positivity with negativity, for that negativity will automatically *negate* the positivity. If you want to say something positive, focus only on the positive.

> *"Insults should be written in the sand, and praises carved in stone."*
>
> – ARAB PROVERB

When you begin a sentence positively, and then add the conjunction 'but', the listener automatically knows that you are going to say something that contradicts the initial positive message. Then, *that person only hears what is said after the 'but'!* The compliment – meant to motivate – is lost. The person is left only with the demotivating criticism, which wasn't your intention at all!

This reminds me of the times when I take my wife out to dinner. I tell her that her dress looks fantastic, her hair is delightful, she looks so young, beautiful and sexy, but I am not sure about those shoes. *Bam!* The only thing that registers is *he doesn't like my shoes*. Somehow, all the other compliments are lost and have evaporated into thin air. And suddenly, she is now disappointed that I don't like her shoes. The result is the opposite of what I wanted; I wanted to make her feel amazing, not doubtful or disappointed.

Julius Caesar knew of the importance of motivation. As a matter of fact, he would learn the names of as many of his soldiers as possible; when the battle was at its fiercest, Caesar would ride close to the front and call out encouragement: "Well done, Flavius! Great shot, Maximus!" As an effective leader, he knew that this positive, personal encouragement would motivate his troops to fight even harder. And it did.

If we want to motivate people through compliments and recognition, we need to focus solely on positive messages. If motivation includes a 'but', an ugly transformation is taking place: motivation morphs into demotivation. If we have suggestions for improvement, that's super. We will get a chance to voice those as well – but later. It's better that we park those, for now, and bring them up at another time.

> *"Instruction does much, but encouragement does everything."*
>
> –WOLFGANG VON GOETHE

Marathon Diary

Concerning this marathon, I'm blessed to say that I feel fantastically motivated. This is thanks to two sources.

One source of motivation comes from my friends on Facebook. On this social platform, I made the public commitment to run the marathon. Thereon, I was bombarded with lots of doubters – who have transformed into lots of cheerleaders! Each day that I run, I post my status, showing how far I've gone (time and/or distance), and each time I am rewarded with lots of 'likes' from my friends. They post positive comments, words that echo in my head and spur me forward. I'm also inspired in realising that I myself, in a way, have become inspirational: many of my friends have started to run in response to my activity!

The other source of encouragement, believe it or not, comes from a machine. I'm in love with my *Nike plus* application. Every time I run this app, it tells me my time and my progress, and it urges me on until I reach my goal for the day. Best of all, if I run further, or for longer, or if I run one of the standard distances (one mile, a 1K, a 5K, or a 10K) as a new personal best, I receive a congratulatory message from a well-known celebrity such as Trey Harding or Lance Armstrong! That always makes me want to beat my personal best.

It's amazing how even the positive messages of encouragement from a mere computer program can serve to motivate us. It just goes to show how receptive we are to praise and how powerful it truly is. Imagine how powerful the words of encouragement from boss, partner, or parent can be!

As for me… another week, another 20km run. Back in the groove after the holiday, running five or six times a week.

Week 16 Distance

Lead by Example

> *"Setting an example is not the main means of influencing others; it is the only means."*
>
> – ALBERT EINSTEIN

Recently, I watched an interview of Sam Mendes concerning *Skyfall*, the latest James Bond film. He was describing how it was such a dramatic and action-packed film; it was so action-packed, in fact, that Mendes had arranged an army of doubles for the leading actors. These doubles would be performing all the major stunts.

Except Daniel Craig's.

Craig performed many of his own stunts, insisting that he had to live the role as much as possible. He felt that it was important – for the sake of the film, for the film's quality – that people saw Bond up close during the action sequences. That wouldn't have been possible with a double. When they were shooting the scenes with Bond fighting on top of a moving train, Mendes tried to persuade Craig to use a double who was already trained for exactly such scenes. Craig asked that they try it with the train moving at 20mph, just to see how it went. It went well. They gradually increased the speeds until he was fighting on top of a train running at 50mph.

Sam Mendes admitted that Craig's choice had an incredible impact on the entire cast and the whole production. It provided everyone with a real leader on set, someone who was setting the tone for the making of the film. Someone who truly believed in the film and believed in his job. Everyone who was involved received a powerful subliminal message: *do your best*. No one wanted to be the person who let everyone else down.

So it goes. The most effective – and genuine – way to lead is to lead by example. Although it is the most beneficial and most powerful approach, we often underestimate its impact and results. As a leader in your organisation, you can have the exact same effect as Daniel Craig did. *You* set the tone, because *you* set the example. The effect will be as positive and dramatic as you make it.

I recall how a company that I was involved in once underwent a massive organisational change. We consolidated and outsourced services to strategic partners, instead of doing the work internally. We also off-shored the work, meaning that we had to significantly change the way we worked and with whom. This transformation was very difficult and resulted in a lot of conflict. There were clashes between my own team and our strategic providers, and also between my own team and the other internal teams. This infighting was a real hindrance to progress. All the time spent fighting was time wasted, which we otherwise could have used to work together to resolve the problems and make actual progress. Needless to say, we were working in a pretty unhealthy environment.

At the start of the following year, I ran a strategy conference. The focus was going to be on collaboration, cooperation and teamwork. This was going to be tough, as the infighting was rife; I was even involved in it myself, to some extent. Yet as the conference approached, we'd created the presentations, designed the workshops, organised the team-building events and the celebration dinner, and conducted everything else that we could think of in order to make the conference a cooperation-promoting success.

When I arrived at the conference, I saw a dear old friend from the United States. Naturally, I went up to him and gave him a big hug, which he reciprocated. This surprised many people, because hugging isn't really something that is common in Germany. And that gave me an idea.

I was going to hug everyone.

> *"The task of leadership is not to put greatness into humanity, but to elicit it, for the greatness is already there."*
>
> – JOHN BUCHAN

I realised that once you hug someone, you have changed the relationship; you have crossed a line and you have extended a connection. If I've hugged you, then asking me for help should be easier; if you know that I already like and appreciate you, approaching me to discuss a difficult topic should not seem impossible. So, I started to hug more and more people. It became a bit of a theme at the conference. I even noticed other people starting to hug each other!

When I stood up to give my keynote speech, one of the key messages was that we needed to stop the infighting. As I got to that message, I added this: that every time someone wanted to fight with me, I was going to hug them. I was going to make the first move to stop this madness and get us moving towards solutions. "It's hard to fight someone who refuses to fight you," I reminded them, "and it's even harder to fight them if they are hugging you."

Everyone laughed. I suppose they thought it was a bit of a gimmick, but I told them I was serious. We had invited our strategic partners to the conference, and I took every opportunity to hug them.

By the end of the three-day conference, everyone was hugging everyone – even my team and the partners. The atmosphere had completely changed; people were being polite and cooperative towards each other, we saw collaboration and communication improving, and there was a tangible spirit of camaraderie developing. Best of all, this newfound camaraderie did not fade. As we progressed through the next year, our results skyrocketed due to our increased teamwork and collaboration.

This was all because people started hugging people! In this situation, I had become the change I had wanted to see. I'd helped promote peace by proving: *I am not going to fight you anymore; I will hug you instead.*

> *"Be the change you wish to see in the world."*
>
> – MAHATMA GANDHI

Marathon Diary

I am a huge advocate of leaders showing the way and often speak of it. But I'm still amazed – OK, floored – by the impact that my running is having. When I moved from Week 2 to Week 3, running six days a week and showing steady progress, friends began messaging me to tell me they thought it was so inspiring that I was running and making such steady progress. Pretty soon the messages changed to: *I've started running myself! Seeing what you have achieved, I have now decided to do it!*

I am just training for a marathon, trying to keep my morale high, trying to reach my goal. 'Setting an example' had not exactly been my initial intent, but it is a beautiful byproduct. But now that I stop and look around, I see that a lot more people have joined me. Even my young daughters decided that they would like to run as well, and they're getting up at 5.30am to train (if you've got teenage daughters, you can empathise; getting these kids out of bed, of their own free will, at 5.30 in the morning is a major achievement!). Over a dozen of my friends and colleagues have taken to the streets and have also committed to run either full or half marathons.

After a couple of 10K and 5K runs to warm up, Tarak and I decided to see whether we could complete 30km. We ran them slow and steady, focusing on completion and not on speed. Completing this distance was another major milestone for us. It also allowed us to practise our eating and drinking while running, finding out what we liked (and could handle) and what we didn't.

Week 17 Distance

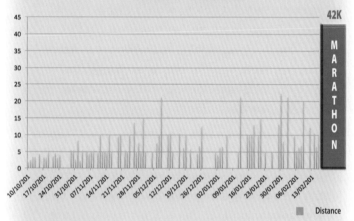

I have sad news.

My good friend Tanya passed away this week. Tanya was my original inspiration and her fight had been the example that I have been following.

She's been battling cancer for three years, and I'm glad she is no longer suffering. She'd moved into a hospice when I'd started my training, and had told me that my running gave her the strength and courage to keep fighting. I'll continue running. I can't stop now.

I've realised that *we must also run for those who cannot.*

MILE EIGHTEEN ...
Reward and Recognition

> "We increase whatever we praise. The whole creation responds to praise, and is glad."
>
> – CHARLES FILLMORE

In many of the companies I have worked for, the policy was that you shouldn't praise people for just doing their job. Why? The logic was that people don't have to be praised for something they're being paid to do; they're expected to do it, so they should deliver no less, right? People don't need to be encouraged or recognised for something they've *got* to do, yes?

No. I cannot subscribe to this type of thinking, which is much more common than it should be.

Consider this perspective: my firm belief is that people's salaries are what they are paid to come to work. Payment is an incentive to show up, not an incentive to get the job done. You can 'force' them to attend, to come to work, to go through the motions, but you cannot 'force' anyone to do a great job. You can lead a horse to water, but you can't make it drink. Your job as the leader is to inspire your team and to motivate them to do a great job – to get that horse to drink.

Motivation begins with recognition. Genuine recognition shows people that you value their contribution. You notice and appreciate what they do. It proves that their work is important to you. Recognition can take many forms, and it may begin with something small. The culture of recognition is the first stepping stone along the way to the creation of a Winning Culture. And the beauty of recognition is that it costs you nothing – *absolutely nothing* – yet the payback can be more than tenfold.

I've heard many people arguing that we shouldn't praise mediocrity. In their opinion, we should only praise outstanding work. But where will that take us? We'll never breed excellence if we sit on our hands and wait for it. You cannot grow a rosebush without cultivating the seed.

Look at how we encourage our children to walk: their first faltering step is met with huge rounds of encouragement and delight. Their first babbled word is a great cause for celebration. No, they didn't just give a winning speech. They may have voiced a syllable. And no, they didn't run a marathon; they took a small step and then they fell. Yet we cheer them on, we call our partners, our friends, our parents to look at this small wonder and of course we encourage our children to try again.

Why do we do that?

It's because we realise that this is the first faltering step – that it's only the beginning, and that it will get much better much faster if we help them with encouragement. It is with our encouragement, our support, and our help that they will be inspired to try again, to take another step, maybe two or three – until eventually, lo and behold, they can walk and even run. Perhaps one day they'll grow up to run a marathon.

Why is our approach so different, then, when it comes to dealing with our teams or colleagues? Why not encourage a first faltering step? You don't need to go overboard, and you certainly shouldn't slip into the slimy terrain of flattery. You can simply and honestly praise the effort and tell them that maybe next time it will get better. It's essential to let people know that you appreciate their efforts, yet you also let them know – in an encouraging manner – that you expect greater results next time, and you'll be there, waiting and ready to encourage them again.

> *"In the best, the friendliest, and simplest relations, flattery or praise is necessary, just as grease is necessary to keep wheels turning."*
> – LEO TOLSTOY

I don't expect everyone to agree with me on this. I am sure there will be many sceptics regarding this approach. Nonetheless, the cycle of reward and progress is something that I have implemented successfully and witnessed on a myriad of occasions at many companies. I believe in it wholeheartedly.

Case in point: one of these companies had taken the initiative to measure the level of service that we delivered to our customers, versus the level that we had committed to deliver. At first, the measured level of service was low and the reports were inaccurate, but the team were prepared at least to measure the reports. Initially, 0% of the services were meeting the required/agreed level. Nearly all of the reports contained errors; this was natural, as the process was new and the team were still learning. So the first round of recognition to the team was in praise of their taking the time and effort to create the reports, to understand the process of measurement, and to produce the reports on time.

For the next month, the level of services meeting the required level was still at 0%. But now, at least, all of the reports produced were accurate, even if they still failed to meet the required level. This time, we provided positive feedback to the team on the accuracy of the reports. This achievement was indeed important to us, because it demonstrated that people were taking the approach seriously and wanted to improve the situation.

Over the next few months, the service quality improved: around 30% of services met the agreed service level. For those individuals whose services met the required level, we provided positive feedback and recognition for their achievement, namely in the form of reviews with their peers and their managers. Consequently, over the following few months, the percentage of services which met the required level rose to over 50%. As we raised the bar, people needed to show more apparent improvement in order to gain recognition.

At last, one team stood out as the first one to have all their services meet the required level for those consecutive three months. To reinforce how important this achievement was for the company, we gave them a small bonus. That bonus also acted as encouragement – the carrot in front of the horse – for the other teams who now looked to improve their performance until all their services were also at the required level.

We continued with this strategy of positive feedback and encouragement. We even set the annual team target, with 80% of the services meeting the agreed level for the entire year. Now everyone had seen that improvement was possible. They knew what was required in order to improve the service and could define the reward for accomplishing the goal.

That year, every single team achieved the target.

And one team, in fact, surpassed it. They reached 100% of the level of service desired. In recognition of that, we celebrated with a small team event to show our appreciation. The following year, we set the target at 90%. Again, all the teams met that target, with some surpassing it. Overall, we achieved a record level of 95%.

This significant improvement all began with us providing recognition to the team for delivering reports which showed that our performance level was rock bottom. The point was not to imply that our performance level needed drastic improvement (though it certainly did). The point was to initiate a culture of recognition, which we did. We provided positive feedback for the small steps, constantly raising the bar, and being all the more selective about what we rewarded and recognised until we had achieved a magnificent performance level of 95%.

Recognition is a tremendously powerful tool. It's like a drilling tool that spears through every wall, used to drive excellent performance and to create a Winning Culture. Reward and recognition are the fuel for the fire of continuous improvement. Don't underestimate that power.

> *"Applaud us when we run, console us when we fall, cheer us when we recover."*
>
> – EDMUND BURKE

Marathon Diary

The *Nike plus* application is one of my favourite sources of reward and recognition. In addition to sending me its congratulatory messages, it also awards small 'prizes' in order to encourage progress. I'm awarded with 'badges' when I run four, five, six, or seven times a week, when I brave poor weather conditions, when I run a 15K or a 20K, and when I run for a number of consecutive weeks.

No big deal, right? They're not real badges, and this application is really only being seen by me. But actually, it *is* a big deal. It serves as a constant reminder of the progress I've made. It's my most faithful cheerleader. And, as the saying goes, if you want something repeated, reward it.

As I am making more progress, the news that I will be running a marathon has spread like wildfire amongst my peers and acquaintances. People are constantly asking me how I'm doing. Most people thought I was aiming for a 10K or a half marathon, and they're surprised to learn that I'm completing the full marathon. Once they get over their initial shock, though, they're proud of me.

It's just one more thing that helps me to keep going.

I've caught an infection that was doing the rounds this week and had to significantly reduce the training. Since I am on antibiotics, I am not supposed to run for ten days, so I've been going on some 5K walks to keep up the rhythm of training. Thankfully, I am ahead of schedule, and this setback doesn't throw me off track, thanks to the policy of *no mañanas*!

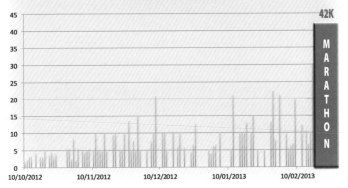

Week 18 Distance

Distance

MILE NINETEEN . . .

Positive Competition

> *"Most people never run far enough*
> *on their first wind to find out*
> *they've got a second."*
>
> – WILLIAM JAMES

Another formula in the creation of a Winning Culture is the ingredient of *positive competition.* The word itself may seem like an oxymoron at first. But if you analyse it for a moment, you'll realise that it's simply about bringing out the best – the most positive elements – in competition.

When I seek to create a Winning Culture in my teams, this is one of my favourite techniques to use. Initially, I seek to create small successes for each team. As soon as that ball begins to roll, I work to get it snowballing. I initiate internal competition between the teams by creating role models who encourage the teams to emulate each other's achievements.

It's a tricky business, granted. This competition needs to be set up in a positive way; if negativity or tensions ensue, the strategy will backfire. Your goal must be to inspire, not to inhibit. You want to look out for all of your teams' members, and help them all to achieve 100%.

You don't want a shining team and an outcast team (or shining member and outcast member, respectively); as a leader, it's your goal to bring everyone to the point where they can reach their fullest potential. It can be a difficult balancing act.

One good technique is by instilling both individual *and* shared goals within these teams. For instance, if you have two teams (Team A and Team B) and your business delivers software, then you give the teams two specific and individual targets. Say, the first target is for each team to accomplish a 90% on-time delivery rate within the business. The second target, which is shared, is to accomplish an overall 90% on-time delivery rate of the software.

Team A may be more dedicated to achieve the internal goal of 90% on-time delivery first. Once they have achieved that, however, they benefit from helping Team B get to 90% as well, since this then helps everyone reach the second target. This approach encourages the right level of competition; both teams will want to be first to achieve the individual target, but once that has been achieved, they will then help each other to also achieve the second target in time. Best practices are shared between the teams as each team benefits through the success of the other team.

We don't want any losing teams; we only want winning teams. That's why it's fundamental to create a win-win strategy and a win-win goal. That's the cornerstone of a Winning Culture. A Winning Culture is not so much focused on the *winning* – for the word itself implies that someone is losing. Instead, it is focused on *success*.

The idea of a Winning Culture is explored and expanded upon in many articles and books. Most authors would agree that such cultures of success have a specific standard: success is the norm; it is not only achieved, but is expected. It is this expectation of success which you must seek to nurture, because it becomes a self-fulfilling prophecy.

Success breeds success.

> *"And while the law of competition may be sometimes hard for the individual, it is best for the race, because it ensures the survival of the fittest in every department."*
>
> – ANDREW CARNEGIE

This is a concept which does not often overlap in the sports world and the business world. Concerning athletics, a Winning Culture is completely team-oriented; there must be solidarity *within a team*, but there is competition *between teams*. The objective is to beat your rival. In a business organisation, however, we need all of our departments, all of our teams, and all of our people to be successful and cooperative in order to achieve optimal performance. If we work together, if we raise ourselves and pull others up with us, and if we set up healthy internal competition, we can breed a win-win mentality that will improve the overall performance.

The key is *healthy* internal competition. If you create winners and losers, you promote jealousy and destructive behaviour, which will obviously have a negative impact on the organisational atmosphere and overall performance. We need to avoid the negative aspects that winning can create: beware the *win at all costs* attitude, look out for situations where people become obsessed or lazy or bend the rules in order to win, and avoid mentalities that foster the notion that winning becomes the be-all and end-all. This can have a corrosive and corruptive influence, and it will end badly.

Instead, create a Winning Culture that is synonymous with *a culture of success*. Focus on creating an organisation that is supportive and welcoming, one that is focused on win-win rather than win-lose, and one that has great and glowing expectations. Your environment should promote the success of each and every team.

But if everyone is a winner, what are we competing against?

In a Winning Culture, your adversary is failure itself. You look to compete against the goals that you set. You're aiming for success; you're not aiming to beat someone else. You're aiming to improve yourself, to personally perform better than you were yesterday. If anything, you're winning against yourself.

This doesn't mean that we eliminate negative elements completely, as there will always be indirect competition anyway. And it certainly doesn't mean that we lower the bar or our expectations. It doesn't mean that we set easier targets. You don't want a culture of mediocrity! The meaning of internal competition, after all, is that the teams measure themselves against the others as they all try to meet their goals.

The difference is the target: the target is the *goal*, not beating the other team. This may seem subtle, but it's a big difference. This is what fosters collaboration and support between the teams. With this alignment, teams also know that they can rely on others should they encounter difficulties. This fosters camaraderie and trust, while also helping to increase their confidence and expectations.

Set it up so that your people need all the teams – not just their own – to be successful in order to attain the full reward. Your teams should be focused on (and proud of) not just personal achievement, but on the overall improvements and developments of the department and the entire business. You must make everyone realise that each person matters and counts. Everyone is a part of a greater success.

"If everyone is moving forward together, then success takes care of itself."

– HENRY FORD

Marathon Diary

I'm witnessing a culture of positive competition inadvertently blossoming around me. This typically happens when someone takes the initiative and starts doing something as relatable and interactive as running. People start noticing, people start following, and eventually people start 'competing'.

My friends now post their own running times and distances; we're encouraged and goaded by the results and accomplishments of others. We push ourselves to run further, longer, or faster. It is all friendly, because our goal is mutual encouragement and progress. I've got a very healthy competition going with Tarak and Dave. When we work out together, we give more of ourselves. The collective training certainly helped on the cold dark mornings in January. Even when we train alone, we push the limit of what has been achieved previously. When one of us reached a new distance – like a 25K – the rest of us are encouraged to try too, since we have proof that it is achievable.

Best of all, as soon as we get back together and run, we look to repeat the new distance together so that we are all at the same level. If any one of us gets too far ahead, this could backfire; it would prevent us from training together since we'll be at different levels. We all want to be the first to run a new distance but, upon completing it, we pause to help the others catch up. We are a team, but we are also individuals, and we need to help each other.

I've never seen them as my competitors. We all share the same goal, we all want to do the marathon, and we all want our friends to complete it with us. This competitive and collaborative effort is what drives our collective improvement. I've watched us go from a best of 10K to 20K, and then on to 25K, and finally on to 30K… and we're still pounding away on the pavement.

Unfortunately for Dave, the Dusseldorf Marathon coincides with the date of his daughter's 10th birthday, so Dave will not be able to run in this marathon. Given our positive competitive spirit, Dave will still continue to run and train with us in order to push the rest of the team closer to our goal.

It doesn't end here! We are keeping our eyes out for another marathon after the one in April, where we in turn can run with Dave to ensure that he has the support he needs to complete the goal, too. And, recovered from the infection, I have taken up running once again! As most of my long runs take place during the weekends, Dave has not been able to join in, so this week we did a long run in the evening to help him break the 25km barrier for the first time.

This is the power of positive competition; it leads to cooperation and collaboration between us so that all of us will ultimately achieve our goals. It is this positive competition which pushes us forward, and which will hopefully keep pushing us until the end.

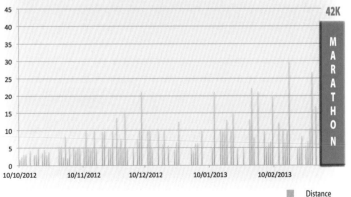

Week 19 Distance

Mistakes: The School of Hard Knocks

> *"Freedom is not worth having if it does not include the freedom to make mistakes."*
>
> – MAHATMA GANDHI

Mistakes are a necessary part of learning and developing. You don't win or lose. You either win or learn. Unfortunately, this mentality isn't upheld by too many companies. How many workplaces do you know which have created an environment that tolerates mistakes? More often than not, people are punished for their mistakes, which consequently teaches them that mistakes are dangerous and must be kept to a minimum. So much for 'learning from your mistakes'.

Yes, mistakes can be costly. Yes, you should look to keep them to a minimum. You needn't encourage mistakes just for the sake of learning. Just be more tolerant of them. When they occur – and they will – work with your teams to minimise the impact and maximise the learning.

If you punish mistakes, you create a culture where risks are avoided, since risk-taking often increases the probability of mistakes and failure. But if you eliminate risks, you really will be settling for mediocrity, since small risks only lead to small gains. As the saying goes, *you have to go out on a limb sometimes, as that is where the fruit is.* In order for your organisation to reach its full potential, you need to take risks. Some of these will be big risks, and this means that you will increase your probability of mistakes and failure. But it also increases your probability of great success and great improvement. If you can embrace this, you'll recognise it as progress.

As a leader, remember that you set the culture. You need to be the one who encourages sensible risk-taking in a safe environment. If you focus on punishing mistakes, then you are freezing progress.

It's not just your own mistakes that you must take into account. Sometimes, the mistakes of others may prove far more beneficial to your learning experience. It runs along the lines of why waste your time reinventing the wheel, when you can just grab it and create a unicycle and go where you need to go? If you dismiss other people's mistakes, you are robbing yourself of some very profound and necessary learning experiences.

When others trip or fumble, we might think: *How stupid. Why did he do that? I would never do that.* We rarely think: *Wow, that's a great lesson. What does that teach me? How could I act differently?* But that's exactly what we should be thinking, if we want to draw anything positive from the experience. Why do we study history? Why do we read biographies? We can learn from the lives of others.

"What do you do when you learn to swim?
You make mistakes, do you not?
And what happens?
When you have made all the mistakes
you possibly can without drowning –
and some of them many times over –
what do you find?
That you can swim?

Well – life is just the same as learning
to swim! Do not be afraid of making
mistakes, for there is no other way of
learning how to live."

– ALFRED ADLER

Unfortunately, we do not always learn. Sometimes we suffer the same mistakes until the lesson is finally (hopefully) drilled into our heads. One of the biggest and most tragic examples of repeated mistakes is the war in Iraq, which marks the US's most current conflict in the world. This is a war that erupted because the United States failed to learn from the lessons of the brutal Vietnam War (the biggest US military disaster until this Iraq War).

You'd have thought that such a costly war – costly in money, energy, time, and lives – would have at least instilled some lessons. But no, the US repeated many of the same mistakes as it had in Vietnam, including:

- ✓ *Underestimating the enemy and their tenacity to throw a foreign occupier from their soil.*
- ✓ *Deceiving the public about how badly the war progressed.*
- ✓ *The initial excessive use of force instead of a plan to win hearts and minds.*
- ✓ *Lacking a 'clear date' for withdrawal of US forces.*
- ✓ *Starting a war with another country for concocted reasons which did not hold up under scrutiny.*

I've written hundreds of *lessons learned reports*, but what have I learned from them? I don't think I've ever been offered a *lessons learned report* by a colleague. The only thing that comes close, I suppose, is that handbook of common mistakes made (FAQ), learned from trial and error. I doubt that most people take the time to even read those.

Learning from mistakes should be a policy and a lifestyle that extends far beyond the professional sphere. Mistakes are an ingredient of life; in your everyday personal life, you have to recognise and learn from them, too. Sometimes, parents and older siblings try to warn us or teach us from their mistakes, but that only works to an extent. I distinctly remember my father warning me: "I wouldn't do it that way, son..." just before I made a complete mess of things (on several occasions).

Later down the line, I remember several occasions when I have tried to let my own son benefit from my multitude of mistakes. But he had to make the same mistakes himself in order to truly learn. It seems that each generation has to make a few of the same mistakes in order to 'learn the hard way.'

I suppose that, sometimes, the hard way is the only way.

> *"The only man who never makes a mistake is the man who never does anything."*
>
> – THEODORE ROOSEVELT

Marathon Diary

Naturally, I've made a number of mistakes during my training for the marathon. And thank goodness I made them. All these mistakes have to be learned in training; if I wait to learn them during the marathon itself, there is no way I will be able to complete the race. Here's a fun handful:

Wearing the wrong clothing (and ending up either too hot or too cold).

- ✓ *Running too fast too soon.*

- ✓ *Eating the wrong foods before running (hello indigestion, and thank you hampered running).*

- ✓ *Not taking proper precautions beforehand, and then trying to work out how to take a toilet break.*

As is often the case, I do have to make many of these mistakes *myself* in order to learn from them. Yes, I'd been advised against some of them. Yes, I'd heard of the more common errors and pitfalls that other joggers make, and yet it seems that I still had to try them out for myself.

Having run shorter distances with no issues, I assumed I was immune to making more mistakes. The thought itself is a mistake. The first time I ran 30km (it happened to be one of the warmer days in the Dusseldorf winter), I noticed a stinging, sticky feeling after just 11km. Yes, I had *jogger's nipple*: it was bleeding. I took off the offending item of clothing and threw it away.

In retrospect, I see how obvious this issue should have been to me: there was a badge woven into the shirt right where the nipple was. I should have noticed that immediately and put the shirt aside, but I didn't. I thought I was immune to any more mistakes. I wasn't. I learned my lesson. And I choose my shirts far more wisely now. The important thing is that I am learning every day.

If you don't make mistakes, you're not trying. If you don't try, you won't learn. If you don't learn, you won't be prepared. And if you're not prepared, you'll be shot down.

This week in training I've decided that I need to know whether I can really do this or not. I want a dress rehearsal. I want to make sure that any mistake I make is going to be during practice for the first (and hopefully only!) time. As a result, I pushed myself to finish 35km, just seven kilometres short of the magical distance.

One of the things I have learned is that whatever distance I decide to run, *it is always the last two kilometres which are the most difficult*. Just two kilometres. It is a purely psychological matter. So before my 35km run, I told myself that I would 'actually' be running 40km. Thus, if the last two kilometres seem too hard, at least I'd already be done with 38km.

It's pretty fantastic how we can trick ourselves if we just put our minds to it!

As I approached the end of the 35km, I felt good! The trick worked. And in fact, I felt so good that I kept going, wondering when my mind or body would ultimately force me to stop. How far *could* I go? Could I run all 42km, a full marathon? Would I hit the dreaded 'wall' before I was done? What would it feel like?

In the end, I didn't hit the wall. I felt good and managed to complete 40km. And I was tempted to run the last two kilometres and complete the full distance, but instead I decided to walk, and save completing the full marathon for the official race. Now I really know that I can do it. Not that I doubted myself before, but… you never know. *Trust, but verify*, as former US President Ronald Reagan used to say.

My running time was 4:48, and I ran nice and easy; if I had run the last two kilometres I am sure I could have finished everything in just over five hours. Given that the target time is under 5:30, I am pretty sure that I can complete the distance within the time limit.

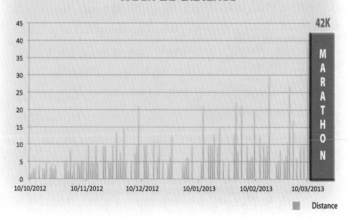

Week 20 Distance

Accountability vs. Responsibility

"It is easier to fight for one's principles than to live up to them."

– ALFRED ADLER

Do you know the difference between *accountability* and *responsibility*? It may seem like the line blurs between the two definitions and, in fact, in many languages it does. The German word for accountable is *verantwortlich*. But guess what? The German word for responsible is also *verantwortlich*.

Tricky.

In English, things don't get much clearer. If you check online, you'll often find interchangeable definitions. But personally, I see a clear enough difference, and I try to explain this distinction to my team to ensure that they understand my expectations. So far, it's worked well for me.

✓ *Responsibility implies involvement; you are devoted to something, possibly you're performing a clearly defined task, and your performance can determine a successful outcome.*

✓ *Accountability means that your performance is what determines a successful outcome. Even if you're not performing any of the respective tasks yourself, even if you're not devoting your time and energy directly, you're still the one 'in charge'. If things go wrong, you are to blame.*

You can find great examples of this distinction anywhere – including, of course, the world of sports. Who is responsible for a football team's success, for instance? The players – because they've got to perform the passing, tackling, attacking, defending and scoring of the goals (all of which determine which team wins the game). But are they *accountable*? No. The manager is accountable for the team's behaviour and results.

If the team loses, the manager is the guy who has to explain *why* to his boss and to the fans in the stands, and he'll suffer the consequences if there's a pattern of poor results. Is this fair? Some people don't think so. After all, the manager doesn't kick the ball even once. So how can he be held accountable? Well, *he is* – because he is the one who selects the players, who trains them, who decides the tactics and provides the motivation and the game plan, and who initiates any changes or improvements as the games unfold.

Another way to distinguish between *responsibility* and *accountability* is this: responsibility can be delegated, but accountability cannot. If you begin trying to delegate accountability, it usually means that you're looking for someone to blame for a failure. The person who is accountable should already know that he or she is accountable, and should act like it.

> *"It is not only what we do, but also what we do not do, for which we are accountable."*
>
> – MOLIERE

As a leader, the type of environment that I try to create is one where my team feel accountable for success and they know that I feel accountable for their failure. I do my best to communicate this to them openly. I start by explaining myself like this: "I know that it's you guys who do all of the actual work, not me. My job is to ensure that you are successful, that you have all the tools and necessary support in order to be successful. If you feel that's not happening, then please let me know and I will address it..."

This is the type of agreement that I seek to create with the team. Credit for success will be given to them or to the individual who delivers the success (and thus deserves it). If problems arise, I (the leader) will help resolve them and will do all that can be done to get the team back on track. More often than not, they truly appreciate this agreement, and I in turn do my best to look out for them. This is an approach and attitude that fosters trust between the leader and the staff, and that makes for a very healthy work environment.

As a leader, remember it is your job to ensure that your people have all the required tools to be successful. It's your responsibility to arm them for success and to work to remove any roadblocks that may stop them being successful. Communicate to them that you know you are accountable, and that you are prepared to be so. Openly telling them this means that you are publically committing yourself to them, and also shows that you are happy to be held accountable for their progress, or lack thereof. It's what you pledge to do anyway, as a leader. So why not communicate it openly to them?

> *"Ninety-nine percent of all failures come from people who have a habit of making excuses."*
>
> – GEORGE WASHINGTON CARVER

I have a professional story to share which can shed some light on this. I remember working for one company which had a pretty bad on-time delivery reputation. The rate was below 30%. I took over the responsibility in this department, so I was keen to improve the situation. As a first step, I implemented some formal project reviews for myself and the other key staff.

To my surprise, this action was not greeted with the enthusiasm I had hoped for. As a matter of fact, several project managers went so far as to approach me and tell me how much they disliked it. They told me that being shot in public for their failure was not going to help improve either the success rate or morale. My reply was that I did not view this as a public execution. This was supposed to be a forum where they could raise issues, highlight problems, and make requests directly to me for support and assistance. In turn, I would do everything I could to help. As I was accountable for the overall situation, I had to be involved in helping to resolve the issues.

Just communicating something as simple as this changed the whole atmosphere and dynamics. Once they realised where I was coming from, how I would help, and what my intentions were, these project managers were suddenly more than happy to attend the meetings.

All except one. One project manager informed me that he wasn't going to come to the review because his projects were on time, on budget, and he was exceeding all quality targets. He didn't feel the need to attend the meeting. I told him that I was disappointed, as it would take away the opportunity for me to say *great job, well done* in front of his peers and his manager... but, of course, it was up to him if he didn't want to come.

He ultimately showed up to the review, where I praised his performance and made him particularly happy.

I realised that the approach I'd adopted in this scenario was valuable because it also ensured that we did not have a 'blame culture'. Instead, we had created a culture where people felt they could raise issues and would get help. This increased the amount of help requested – not the amount needed, but the amount *requested*. Moreover, it also encouraged people to ask for help earlier, as they came to the realisation that they would indeed be helped, rather than blamed.

Previously, I'd been informed of issues only when it was too late to do anything. Now the issues were being raised in time for corrective action and we usually had more than enough time to turn things around. Not surprisingly, we increased the on-time delivery rate from less than 30% to over 80%.

It was fantastic.

> *"We are made wise not by the reconciliation of our past, but by the responsibility of our future."*
>
> – GEORGE BERNARD SHAW

Marathon Diary

In light of this marathon, I feel fully accountable for my success, or lack thereof. I have a realistic plan. I have identified the time I need to do the training. I have the right aspirations, inspirations and motivations. I have some wonderful training partners to push me out of my warm bed to run in the cold dark mornings.

All I need to do is to apply myself, to ensure that I don't over-train, and to keep myself as healthy as possible… all of which is possible. At this moment,

I have even run 40K in training! Not many people have dared to do that, so I know that I'm ahead of the game and that I can do this. I just have to keep training for three more weeks, and give it my all on the day of the actual marathon.

Yes, it's been tough. Yes, I got sick for a while and had to cut myself some slack. But the great thing is that I've prepared for these setbacks; I had looked to get ahead of the plan so that I could mitigate anything (like an illness) that would try to hold me back. *Hope for the best, but plan for the worst,* as the saying goes... I couldn't have phrased it better myself.

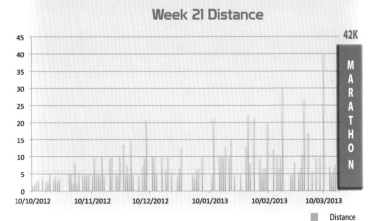

Week 21 Distance

The Law of the 5 Ps

> *"Success depends upon previous preparation, and without such preparation there is sure to be failure."*
>
> – CONFUCIUS

Proper Preparation Prevents Poor Performance: otherwise known as **The Law of the 5 Ps**. That happens to be one of my favourite sayings. The truth of that phrase has been validated time and time again. We humans have proven – personally, professionally, in all spheres of life – that the thing which stops us from performing at our best is, more often than not, a lack of preparation rather than a lack of ability.

Hopefully, you've prepared for many things in your life, and ideally you'll prepare for many more. When you're studying for a university exam, that's preparation. When you're rehearsing a presentation at work or a play for the local drama club, that's preparation. When you're planning a project or doing risk analysis, that's preparation. When you're going through potential questions and answers in your mind before a job interview, that's preparation. When you're stopping by the grocery store to buy ingredients in order to cook a meal before your stomach starts growling, that's preparation.

Preparation requires focus. You need to consider thoughtfully the task at hand, ensure that you're clear about it, and so forth. The more you prepare, the better you'll be able to deal with both the expected and the unexpected. Focusing and analysing help to increase your understanding, and thus your capability and your confidence. Given capability and confidence, your performance is far more likely to be successful.

If you plan to succeed, you must succeed in planning.

> *"Practice makes perfect."*
>
> – ENGLISH PROVERB

This is no revolutionary notion. One of the main reason behind the military success of the Roman Empire was the 'secret' of their outstanding preparation. The Romans regarded training as an absolute necessity in their preparation for war. In their eyes, warriors were not born; warriors were made. Their intense training programmes upheld and reflected this mindset.

From the very beginning, a Roman recruit was drilled relentlessly, which simultaneously strengthened him physically and acquainted him with the tools of war. Once the new soldier had acquired proficiency with his individual weapons, he joined in the various unit level exercises, which ranged from civil engineering projects to actual battle drills. The purpose of all of these procedures was to ensure that the soldier was completely prepared for battle.

The Roman trainings simulated the battles as closely as possible, and they ensured that all new weapons and tactics were used extensively in training before any real fighting took place. Because of their thoughtful and rigorous preparation, the Roman troops were almost always the best prepared and the readiest in the heat of battle. The Romans understood, practised, and enjoyed the benefits of the maxim *proper preparation prevents poor performance.*

> *"...They have never any truce from warlike exercises... for their military exercises differ not at all from the real use of their arms... nor would he be mistaken that should call those their exercises bloodless battles, and their battles bloody exercise."*
>
> – JOSEPHUS V

Marathon Diary

If I need to be anything, I need to *be prepared*.

In terms of being prepared, I have to know what to expect, to understand it, and to train for it accordingly. That means I have to respect the distance. A marathon isn't just something I decided to do one random morning when I woke up. In order to succeed, I need to be mentally and physically prepared for it.

I need to have a plan for how I am going to run the race. I need to have determined a pace that will keep me going till the finish line. I need to have the right clothing and footwear to ensure that I don't suffer from blisters or irritation. I need to know how I'm going to consume food and water along the way, because it's not possible to run for over four hours without eating or drinking. I need to know when to partake in which sources of energy and how to rehydrate.

Otherwise, I will fail.

> ## "Great minds have purposes; others have wishes."
>
> – WASHINGTON IRVING

Taking the example of the Roman training into account, I want my own training to mirror that mindset: just as they tried to make their practices as realistic as possible, I incorporate as much as I can of the 'real' marathon into my training. For instance, I eat and drink the products that I will use in the race, to see if my body can handle them and process them properly. I try different brands and flavours of energy drinks to figure out which one works best for me.

You might be thinking: *Really? You need to micromanage this much, Gordon? I mean, flavours?*

Yes, actually. During the 2004 Athens Olympic marathon, Paul Tergat – Silver Medallist in the 2000

Sydney Olympics – missed his water point and drank water supplied by organisers. He was accustomed to drinking water at room temperature. The organisers supplied cold water, which gave Tergat cramps. As a result, he finished *tenth*. So yes, the small details are important.

I tried different outfits – shoes, socks, jogging pants, tee-shirts, sweatshirts, underwear, waterproof gear – until I found what I was most comfortable with, and I try to use that in the majority of my runs. As I get closer to the race, I try to do my weekend runs at the same time that the actual race will be, so I can practise what I will eat beforehand. I try to run in a variety of weather conditions in case it rains or snows or gets really hot on the day of the race. Hey, you never know.

Finally, I'm planning to run in an organised half marathon as well, which will give me the experience of running with a crowd. I don't want my full marathon to be the first time when I experience issues like organisation and space and the distractions of other runners (difficult to recreate in personal training).

As part of the training this week, I did a fitness assessment to judge my preparation so far. I see that my capability is improving because I'm able to run longer distances and for longer times, but I need to know where my cardio fitness is at. The cardio test involves running hard for 30 minutes, at the fastest pace you can sustain. It then measures your heart rate during the run, and then it measures it again during the two minutes of recovery to see how quickly your heart rate returns to normal.

I'm happy and relieved to say that my test results are great. The rating is based on the speed of recovery; within those two minutes after running flat-out, my heart rate was almost back to its resting level. My fitness rating is 100% (obviously, this is calibrated to reflect my age, so don't look so surprised). I have also managed to increase my maximum heart rate: from 168, it's now up at 176. This increases the rate for each heart rate zone by about 10bpm, which means that I can run faster and still remain in the desired aerobic zone. Even better – and this does take me by surprise – I actually increased my personal best time by almost two minutes (25 min, 58 sec) for the 5K; this improvement came by running 'slow and steady' in my training. The philosophy of 'run faster by running slower' actually works.

The sports world has its own spin on the mantra that the Romans so appreciated. Athletes like to say: *Train hard, run easy.* And this is definitely my philosophy. I don't want to run hard – it's not my point to finish first in the marathon – but I do want to run easy.

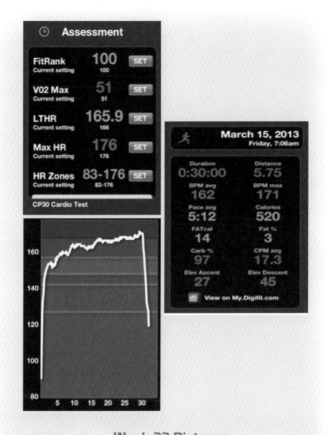

Week 22 Distance

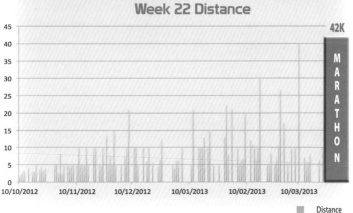

Distance

MILE TWENTY THREE...

Plan, Plan, Follow the Plan

> *"Willing is not enough, we must do."*
>
> – JOHANN VAN GOETHE

The one thing worse than not planning? Spending all your time and energy in planning something to perfection... and then never even following through with the plan! I've seen this happen too many times. People get ahead of schedule, they think everything is on track, they get overconfident, and then they slip. When they try to get back on track, they get delayed or they realise that they've crossed the budget or something else pops up.

It doesn't matter if the issue is a project schedule or a project approach – the only way you'll stay on top of things is if you stick with the programme.

I am a strong believer of *Plan, Plan, Follow the Plan*. After all, if you care enough to create a thoughtful and detailed plan, then the least you can do is follow it, right? It does take effort to keep the plan up-to-date, and it may be challenging to revamp your strategy to clear the hurdles that arise. But it's a worthwhile investment. This is the only thing which will enable you to maintain progress in the desired direction. It's dangerous to let early successes give you a false sense of victory. If you delude yourself like that, it's too easy to stop following up or monitoring the plan. When you stop monitoring, you might as well be quitting. If the approach is working well, remain faithful and stick to it. It's still easy to let things slip.

There are many anecdotes of athletes regarding someone who becomes overconfident: he or she drops the game plan, and then drops out of the game. Light Heavyweight boxing champion Billy Conn is one such famous example.

This champ fought against Heavyweight champion Joe Louis for the title. Conn would not gain weight for the challenge against Louis, deciding instead that he would rely on his tried-and-tested 'hit and run' strategy. Conn was a clever fighter; he was like a mosquito, stinging and moving away before the other guy knew what (literally!) hit him.

For most of that famous game, Conn's strategy was working. He had the upper hand through the first 12 rounds, and was ahead on two of three boxing scorecards. According to many experts and fans who watched the fight, Conn was definitely outmanoeuvring Louis up to that point, because Louis simply couldn't get close to him.

Then... a move that Conn would regret for the rest of his life: *he changed his strategy.*

Instead of using his special 'hit and run' tactic, he tried to go for the knockout in Round 13. This gave Joe Louis the chance he had been looking for. Louis had the upper hand when it came to knockouts. So it was he who knocked out Billy Conn in the 13th round.

Joe Louis won that fight.

Ten minutes after the game's end, Conn admitted to the reporters: "I lost my head and a million bucks." If Billy Conn had stuck to his strategy, he would have made boxing history. He would have become the first Light Heavyweight to win the Heavyweight Title, and he would have done so by beating one of the greatest boxers of all time, Joe Louis. Instead, he'd let his overconfidence overpower and blind him, and he veered away from his trusted plan.

If you want to be victorious, create a realistic plan that you believe in and follow it until you succeed. Don't shoot yourself in the foot.

"No man fears what he has seen grow."
– AFRICAN PROVERB

Marathon Diary

As the marathon looms on the horizon, I feel pretty good. I feel good because I feel very confident. Which is great.

And a little worrying.

I don't want to cross the line into overconfidence. I am very confident right now, and my friends are also very confident in me. They've expressed this and have even suggested that I should aim for running a marathon in less than four and a half hours (even less than four hours, says one guy).

I resist that. Because even though I think I *can* do it, it's not what I *want* to do. It's not my plan. It isn't what I've been training for, and it won't define 'success' for me. For me, success means completing the marathon in less than five hours and 30 minutes… and finishing with a smile.

My dear friends Kristen and Simon repeat two mantras: *Respect the distance; respect your body,* and: *Any marathon you finish healthily is a good marathon.* Wise words…

To do that I want to run this race based on my target heart rate: that means keeping it at an average of 155 beats per minute (bpm), which means that my time should be between five and five and a half hours. This heart rate is important to me, because this is my personal balance between speed and endurance running (aka in the green zone). This is what will allow me to finish in good health and good cheer!

If I try to run faster and set a target of, say, four hours 30 minutes, then I'll probably run spectacularly for a while but run out of steam long before the end. And after so many months and so much preparation and hard work, that would be a bitter defeat indeed. My personal best is about completing the marathon in the manner in which I have trained.

As part of my training, I'm participating in the Bonn Half Marathon (just two weeks before the Dusseldorf

Marathon), to ensure that I can control my adrenalin and stick to the pace and the plan. I've heard that many people who have prepared very well for the marathon lose their heads on the day of the race because they get caught up in the emotion of the event. When the starter says *go,* they kick off as if they're racing Usain Bolt for the 100m Olympic Gold medal. With crowds cheering on from the sidelines, you have to fight the urge to speed up.

I need to learn to ignore the emotion of the moment. I must keep calm and stay focused. If people pound past me and race off out of sight, that's OK. I'm not racing against them; I'm racing against myself. My goal is to complete the marathon. And who knows? I might run by them later, more relaxed and energetic than they, because I am the Tortoise.

Week 23 Distance

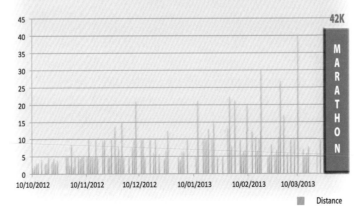

MILE TWENTY FOUR...

Redefining Possible!

> *"The eagle does not catch flies."*
>
> – LATIN PROVERB

There's no such thing as the 'impossible'. Break down the word and realise it for yourself: *I'm + possible.* For years, people believed that it was physically impossible to run a mile in under four minutes. No one had ever done it before, according to all available records. Clearly, it was impossible. At the very least, it was considered very dangerous. Could a person survive such a strain?

Yes. Roger Bannister proved that it could be done. He broke the four-minute mile barrier in 1954, with a time of 3:59.04. And just like that, he redefined what was possible. What's even more amazing is that a mere 46 days after Bannister had achieved this amazing feat, the record was broken again. Jim Landy beat Bannister's time, finishing at 3:58.0. They would both go on to break the record again.

When one person redefines possible, it opens the door to everyone.

This is a leader's mission. It is your duty to open these doors. You must set big, bold, inspiring goals for yourself and for your teams. Possibly these are goals that were previously seen as improbable – even 'impossible' – but, in truth, they are not unattainable. With the right planning, proper preparation, dedication, and determination, they can be achieved.

Remember that once you achieve these goals, you've redefined the baseline of what's possible. A breakthrough *breaks through* a wall and reveals a whole new world of possibilities. Since Roger Bannister achieved the sub-four-minute mile, 1,175 people have followed in his footsteps and achieved the sub-four-minute mile. The current world record is 3:43.13 – a full 17 seconds faster than Bannister's original time.

> *"The greater the difficulty, the more the glory in surmounting it."*
>
> – EPICURUS

So it goes with our teams. Once you help them achieve a big goal, you have instilled a new belief of what is possible and what they are capable of. This cultivates confidence in their own abilities and potential, allowing them to try harder and more fearlessly. It cultivates self-respect for overcoming something difficult, camaraderie for pulling through together, and open-mindedness when it comes to accepting new bold goals.

At another firm where I worked, on-time delivery had wallowed at around a 30-35% success rate. We were horribly behind. I proposed a goal of a 70% success rate for on-time delivery, and it wasn't exactly greeted with enthusiasm. People thought the target was impossible. Still, the team agreed to try; we knew some of our weak points and we had some proposed solutions. We had nothing to lose.

We met our goal. In fact, we exceeded it. We hit an 81% on-time delivery rate. Have redefined the possible – having redefined what *we* were capable of – we tackled two new goals the following year: a target of a 90% on-time delivery rate, and a reduction of major system outages by 40%. Both goals were aggressive, improbable… yet they were successfully completed.

Best of all, when the year swung round again and it was time to set new big, bold and beautiful goals, we were ready with new dreams and goal proposals. Setting and meeting aggressive goals became a habit.

There is no stopping us now!

> *"Fall seven times and get up eight."*
>
> – JAPANESE PROVERB

Marathon Progress

This week was a double celebration. First, Tarak and I completed our first official race, the Bonn Half Marathon. I ran conservatively, running at 'my marathon pace', trying to simulate the marathon. I noted how the race is organised, what the logistics of the start are, how to consume drinks, and what it feels like when people run past me (it's a challenge to stick to my plan and not to chase after them!).

We need to maintain our discipline, our focus, and our plan. Tarak and I completed the Bonn Race within a respectable time (2:18), finishing before two-thirds of more than 4,200 runners!

The chart below shows my heart rate during the race: I achieved the average of 153bpm (in the green zone – yes!) and, more importantly, I was able to maintain it and didn't get caught up in the excitement of the moment. I spent a bit longer in the yellow zone than I wanted, but it was a great workout overall.

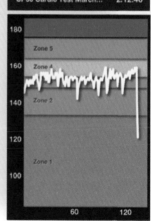

In other news, I've also passed the major milestone of completing 1,000km in training. I know it's no more significant than 999km or 1,001km, but the number is symbolic for me, and I am very happy to have achieved it. Running a marathon *and* a total of 1,000km? Six months ago, had you told me that I would accomplish these two things, I would have told you: *you are crazy*.

But that would have been then. Now, I've redefined what's possible.

So, what's next? This is it. I've got a week left before the actual marathon. In total, I've run over 1,000km in training. I've run eight half marathons, and done runs of 25km, 30km and 40km. I feel ready and prepared. In just six months, look how far I've come – how far anyone can come: I couldn't run 5km without the aid of medics… and now I'm on the verge of completing my first-ever marathon.

I realise that I feel this good because I've actually managed to redefine what is personally possible.

What's next? Oh, trust me – it'll be another big, bold, beautiful goal, that's for sure. But I will have to aim higher than where I am now. I'm no longer at the foothills of a mountain; I've reached the summit, and I'm glancing back at the climb I've done. It's time to find and scale another mountain.

When I mentioned this to my wife, she asked me: "Why don't you make a film?"

I enjoyed a good laugh from that… until I realised she wasn't entirely joking. "What are you talking about? There is no way I could make a film."

She just smiled. "Six months ago you didn't think you could run a marathon. Six months ago you didn't think you could write a book. Look at you now."

She has a point. What previously seemed beyond reach is now within my grasp. So why not dream of other things which I would like to do but didn't ever think I could do? I suppose that once you dare to dream and have achieved a dream, *achieving dreams* should become the norm.

A film. Now that's an idea…

Week 24 Distance

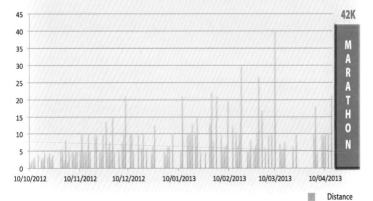

MILE TWENTY FIVE ...

It's Not Over Till the Fat Bloke Runs

*"When I let go of what I am,
I become what I might be."*

– LAO TZU

What does it mean to *win*?

I'd say that we're obsessed with the word. We use it often, almost always with positive connotations; 'winning' is one of the mantras of successful people. A *win* means a 'victory', and it is also a word that has titled a multitude of books, radio stations, music bands, songs, software applications, political parties, and company acronyms. Little wonder. If you want your organisation to succeed, *winning* should be the first word on your agenda. *Winning* should be a habit and a mindset. *Winning* should be the ultimate goal.

It doesn't matter what you're striving to win 'against'. You could be competing against other companies, against project deadlines, or even against yourself. After all, as the saying goes, the one person you can be sure of bettering (beating) is the person you were yesterday. The battles never end, and there's always another win to strive for.

In your organisation, just as in your mind, you must cultivate a Winning Culture. If you foster such a culture, winning becomes a habit, and then a reality. People rise to their expectations; if you motivate them to win every time, then they will try to find a way to win. The problem begins when people take their focus away from winning. Either because they don't realise how important the goal is, or they don't believe themselves capable, or they no longer care. It doesn't matter; the results are the same (and they're bad). If you do not work for success, it will not work for you.

In the sports world, for instance, "I played well but lost" or "We played decently but didn't shoot any goals" is not the equivalent of winning. I agree that playing with integrity is unfailingly better than playing without morals. I am in no way promoting cheating or underhand tactics or anything of the sort. But the fact is, at the end of the day, the scoreboard shows the results.

You win or you lose. Which one is it? We need to be honest with ourselves.

In my sporting days, I played a lot of rugby. I remember when people would often say: "We won, but it wasn't pretty." Why, because they had grass-stains and nose-bleeds from falling down? Well, you don't have to be the most graceful or mind-blowingly stylish winner. You don't have to succeed with flying colours. Any colours will do. In my opinion, there is no such thing as an ugly win or a gracious defeat. Your point is to win, and you either accomplish it or you don't.

> *"The first man gets the oyster;*
> *the second man gets the shell."*
>
> – ANDREW CARNEGIE

In May 2012, Chelsea won the Champions League Final against Bayern Munich. Munich were obviously more talented and attractive on the field, they played 'better', and they appeared to be the much better team. None of that changes the fact that Chelsea still took home the trophy.

Why? Because Chelsea did what they needed to do to win: their focus was simply on winning. They envisioned it, they worked for it, they poured their all into it – and they did it. What I'm saying is: *get the results and meet the objectives you set for yourself.* Don't worry about whether they were done with the style and grace you were hoping for; that's extra, and you can perfect your style later after you've achieved your results.

Great results. That's the goal. Playing gracefully, with style and pizzazz, *and losing*, doesn't cut it – no great results there. Don't believe me? Just ask the Bayern Munich players. They would have much rather played less gracefully, focused just on winning, and won.

When you are focused on winning, that's when you can promote that Winning Culture. Later, once that culture is created, you can adjust yourself to then focus on improving the quality of performance, and the beauty of the way you do things. But improving your style should not come at the cost of winning. If you're playing soccer, it is more important to shoot a goal than it is to look like you're dancing while you're running. You can be sweat-streaked, dirt-smudged, and maybe you're limping, but you're still a victor. If you don't break a sweat and you just show off your techniques or your toned body on the field, and don't make any goals, that won't mean anything.

Focus on the win; everything else should be secondary. It's not about style, it's not about appearance, and it's not about looking good. Of course, many times you'll be tempted to think that's what it's all about. You'll hear other teams telling you: "Sure you won, but it was ugly" or "Yes, you're the victor, but you looked pathetic."

They're trying to get you to change your focus. Don't listen to them. Don't lose your grip on that winning attitude.

> *"If the wind will not serve,*
> *take to the oars."*
>
> – LATIN PROVERB

As an Englishman who loves his sport, I've noticed that this mentality had plagued England for years, especially in the rugby and cricket fields. Our national objective seemed to be 'to at least lose with style'; it wasn't 'we must win'! Guess what? Once we learned to play with the same determination as the All Blacks and the Australians, our fortune changed. We developed a winning attitude, a winning spirit, and ultimately created a Winning Culture which allowed us to win World Cups in both sports, and a host of Gold Medals at the Olympics.

One of my all-time favourite footballers is Billy Bremner. As former captain of the Leeds United football team during their glory days, he led them to win many trophies. They won the League twice, the FA Cup, the League Cup, and the UEFA Cup twice, and yet Bremner's autobiography was titled *You Get Nothing For Being Second.* His point is that, in spite of all their success, his team had not achieved what they set out to achieve. Too often, they stumbled at the final hurdle, losing to opposition that they should have beaten, and ultimately they finished as the runners-up.

In the 1972-73 season, Leeds United were in outstanding form; up to the last month of the season, they were the favourites to win the League, the FA Cup, and the European Cup Winners' Cup. This would make Leeds the first team to win such a treble in the entire history of English football. They'd put themselves in a fantastic position.

Until that last month. Leeds United faltered.

They lost their focus. They started to lose league games... and their grip on the title. Within the last two weeks of the season, Leeds lost two Cup Finals (1-0), against teams, that in my opinion, they should have beaten. In what should have been their greatest season, they ended up trophy-less. Try to imagine all that hard work. All those expectations. All that crumbling confidence and fumbling focus. All that time and energy going down the drain. Sure, they came in second. But what had they desired? They wanted to be first. They lost their focus on winning, and they failed to win.

> *"You can't fail if you don't climb.*
> *But there's no joy in living your*
> *whole life on the ground."*

– ANONYMOUS

Marathon Diary

The saying is: *It's not over until the fat lady sings.*
My version is: *It's not over until the fat bloke runs!*

All the preparation, all the training, all the running in the dark in sub-zero temperatures… that will all have been for nothing if I do not cross the finish line before the five hours and 30 minutes time limit on 28 April. If that doesn't happen, I will have failed.

Yes, I have completely changed my lifestyle. Good things have happened. I'm healthier. I'm running four to six times a week, which would have been unbelievable a few months ago. I have become an inspiration to some of my friends. But for me, all of that is secondary in the face of this goal. My goal is to win. To complete the marathon. To support my friends and help raise that money. If I fail myself in that, I know that I'll feel that failure very deeply.

I will not feel that it has been a great effort, a valiant effort, or that I did my best. I will not pat myself on the back and say, *It's OK, Gordon, you tried. Next time. Fail again. Fail better.* No. I will feel one thing and one thing only. That I have failed, that I have not achieved what I set out to achieve.

My goal is to run the marathon.

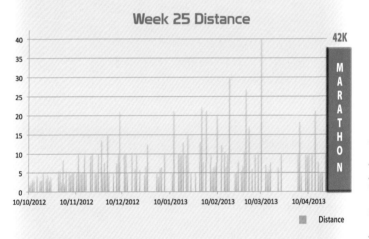

Week 25 Distance

My Final Week training plan:

Sunday:	*Jog for 120 mins.*
Monday:	*Jog for 15 mins, walk for 5 mins, jog for 10 mins.*
Tuesday:	*Jog for 45 mins.*
Wednesday:	*Jog for 70 mins.*
Thursday:	*Jog for 15 mins, walk for 10 mins.*
Friday:	*Walk for 15 mins.*
Saturday:	*Rest Day*

Then Sunday, the day all this has been leading up to… Race Day!

MILE TWENTY SIX...

Success is a Journey, Not a Destination

> *"Do not follow where the path may lead. Instead, go where there is no path and leave a trail."*
>
> – RALPH WALDO EMERSON

It is nearly time. I am no longer counting down the months or weeks. It's a matter of days now. It's a matter of hours. And, when all's said and done, it's all a matter of mind over matter.

To be honest, I hesitated in writing this chapter. Initially, I didn't want to write it until the race was over. Whether my motives were superstitious or symbolic, it doesn't matter now. Now I am writing it. Because I realise that I've already been successful. I'm not done – perhaps no one really is – but I'm a victor. Whether I complete the marathon or not, I've just realised that the real success here is the undertaking of this journey that I have embarked upon. That is the ultimate purpose and triumph... not the finishing of a race on a particular day.

Success is not a one-time event. You need to cultivate a habit, a pattern, a culture of success – this is true success, *sustainable* success. You don't get it by luck or good fortune; it's the result of hard work and fierce desire. True success is not a one-hit wonder, a sole good business year, a stroke of luck in the casino. True success is something that can be achieved even when the odds are against you, something that you create for yourself, and is not merely given to you. Success is a journey because it is about creating sustainable changes which lead to sustainable results.

Along this journey, I've fought, I've slipped, I've got up and triumphed and I've grown. I have proven to myself what I am capable of. With an alignment of aspiration, inspiration, and the right level of determination, I feel that I'm running on the right track. I feel capable of so much, now. Running on this road – literally and figuratively – has helped me travel towards a new horizon, opening my eyes to possibilities and personal potential.

Had you asked me once (before I started training), I would have told you that Gordon Tredgold could never run a marathon, for any number of reasons. I wasn't fit enough, I wasn't an athlete, I didn't have the time... the list of excuses would have been endless. But what I have proven to myself is that it doesn't matter what I have done or thought before. The question is what I'm doing now. Am I working towards a goal? The time it takes to get there shouldn't matter; the time will pass anyway. The future is there for me to shape for myself.

My Marathon Journey has given me a number of blessings. And yes... I will take this moment to count them. And celebrate them. For that is the example that every leader must set, too. Ensure that your team celebrate their successes. Remember, it's a twofold strategy: this lets people know that you've all achieved what you've set out to do, and it's also the reward that motivates and propels future progress.

✓ *The marathon has allowed me to raise money for the Macmillan Cancer Charity, and to show support and solidarity to my friends going through chemotherapy.*

✓ *My health has improved drastically. I feel so much stronger and fitter. My resting heart rate has dropped by over 15 beats a minute. The health and fitness of my fellow runners Dave and Tarak have improved significantly as well. None of us have ever been quite this fit before!*

✓ *I have a much better understanding of training techniques and also of what my body is capable of.*

✓ *I have a much better understanding of inspiration, having been inspired by many people throughout my training, yet also by providing inspiration to others.*

✓ *Running has become a therapy for me; I've found in it a good way to relax, a mind-clearing and meditative method that also provides me with a window of opportunity to think about my life and strategise my days.*

✓ *Running fosters a great sense of camaraderie and friendship. It's been a wonderful experience running with Dave and Tarak.*

We've also befriended many other runners. Experiencing the spirit and mood at the half marathon was an extremely special experience, and it's something that I want to participate in and contribute to again.

✓ *I've reunited with some old friends, Simon and Kristen, whom I hadn't seen for many, many years.*

✓ *I have completed my very first book; the marathon and the preparation provided me with a unique and wonderful framework.*

✓ *I am not afraid to take on new challenges, especially in areas where I have little or no expertise.*

✓ *I have earned a new sense of respect from friends and colleagues who are surprised at my achievement (this includes self-respect, for I initially didn't think myself capable, either!).*

✓ *I have set new, great expectations. Folks are now asking me: What's next? What's next, indeed? We'll soon see! It's a delicious feeling to know that you can move on to the 'next' dream, and aim for a higher mountain!*

I've sweated and stumbled and fought for this success – I've even literally bled for it – and I know what it tastes like. As expected, as in any other significant battle in life, it's been tough going. But ultimately, it has been worth it. And I may be finishing up a marathon, but life's race is far from over. My marathon journey is only the start – the first stepping stone, the very first mile – of a long, beautiful, promising journey of struggle and success.

You cannot fail if you do not give up. Fear nothing. Keep running. And don't stop until you can fly over every hurdle in your path.

The future is yours for the shaping!

Tarak and me, nearly halfway there, running with big smiles!

Kristen, Tarak and me with our medals. Kristen was particularly pleased, as she had every right to be – she had just knocked 15 minutes off of her personal best time!

> *"Whether you think you can or you think you can't, you are usually right."*
>
> – HENRY FORD

That's right, Mr. Ford. I couldn't have put it any better myself!

First, I need to support Dave with completing his marathon, as promised – especially after all the support he has given me throughout the year. So... the next goal is to run together in the Cologne Marathon this coming October!

After my success in Dusseldorf, I have also persuaded several other colleagues to run with me in Cologne. Most will be running their first half marathon, but some will also join us in the full marathon. I am sure that when they cross the finish line, they will taste that sweet, impeccable joy of achievement.

However, I don't want my running to end after these two marathons. To ensure that I continue with the training and all the benefits that come with it, I have set myself a new goal. It's what I call 5-in-5. The goal is to run five marathons in five continents with a target to complete this by the end of 2015...

After a brief review of the various marathons – and a discussion with my wife to see where she would like to visit! – these are the ones I've settled for:

Vancouver Marathon	*May 2014*
Cape Town Marathon	*September 2014*
Hong Kong Marathon	*February/March 2015*
Sydney Marathon	*September 2015*

I already have a group of friends who want to run with me, including Kristen, Simon, Tarak and Mithun... hopefully we will be able to persuade Dave to run as well. The plan has an additional bonus: it will allow us to celebrate Kristen's 50th birthday in Cape Town, while Simon and I will celebrate our 55th birthdays in Sydney!

Finally... who knows? The future is ours for the shaping. Maybe I will live to break the record of the Oldest Marathon Runner. I hope to be running in September 2061, at the age of 101.

How's that for big, bold and beautiful?

About the Author

Gordon Tredgold is a specialist in Transformational Leadership with extensive global and international experience gained from leading large-scale transformation programmes for blue chip companies.

Gordon is a natural leader who has a simple and practical approach to leadership that allows people and organisations to invest quickly in the process and deliver outstanding results.

Gordon was born in Leeds, Yorkshire. He gained a BSc (Hons) in Mathematics at Manchester University and has lived and worked in UK, Belgium, Holland, Czech Republic, USA and Germany.

www.leadership-principles.com/en/

www.facebook.com/LeadershipPrinciples

The Journey Continues . . .

Kristen's story:

My life changed in August of 2003.I had no symptoms, no family history, was young, healthy and physically fit – yet was diagnosed at age 38 with stage IIIC ovarian cancer. Ovarian Cancer has changed my life. Strangely, I am glad that it was I that was diagnosed and not someone else. I do feel as if I have been chosen for this disease. As a result of my diagnosis I have been given the encouragement, strength and motivation to use my ovarian cancer journey as a way to raise awareness, provide education and to raise funds to advance ovarian cancer research towards early detection and eventually a cure.

Since August of 2003, I have been actively involved in many ovarian cancer organizations, both nationally and locally. I am committed to ovarian cancer – not for me but for all women. My mission is to prevent other women from my same fate. I was instrumental in getting the survivors speaking to medical school students started in

Philadelphia in Jan 2004, starting fundraising opportunities such as the teal ovarian cancer "OverCome" awareness bands, Bunco for Ovarian Cancer, Teal Ribbon Night (Ladies' Night Out to play Bunco in Maryland), Lunch and Learn for the Red Hat Society in Ocean City, NJ and the Memorial Day Sunday Teal Ribbon 5k run/walk. I was a runner prior to my diagnosis and for me creating, organizing and hosting the 5k was a dream come true.

Ovarian Cancer is bigger than us all. I do not want another person, another family to have to hear the terrifying words – you have or someone in your family has ovarian cancer. Unfortunately, the general population is not aware of the signs and symptoms of ovarian cancer and ovarian cancer research is underfunded.

As a way to raise funds to further scientific research, in September of 2005, my sister, Karlyn Kay and I co-founded a 501 (c) (3) foundation, Teal Ribbon Ovarian Cancer Foundation, Inc. (TROCRF). TROCRF is organized exclusively for charitable & scientific purposes. Our goals are to raise funds to advance ovarian cancer research towards a cure; advocating for early diagnostic treatment programs and to improve the lives of ovarian cancer survivors.

I am employed full-time with First Data in Wilmington, DE in the Debit Card Services Division. I have been in the electronic funds industry for 30 years. I earned my BS degree from Neumann University, Aston PA in May 2003.

My very supportive family and friends make all things possible. I live in Glen Mills, PA with my wonderful husband, Simon, and incredible 22 year-old daughter; Kimberly. I have become a ultra runner post ovarian cancer. In the last 5 years I have run 11 marathons and two 50k ultra trail races. Life is good! I love life and am thankful it's not a sprint but a marathon!

Kristen, Tarak and me with our medals. Kristen was particularly pleased, as she had every right to be – she had just knocked 15 minutes off of her personal best time!

Notes/References

MILE ONE
http://history.nasa.gov/moondec.html

MILE TWO
http://en.wikipedia.org/wiki/Julio_César_Chávez
http://en.wikipedia.org/wiki/Alex_Ferguson

Faruja Singh
http://www.youtube.com/watch?v=gCY0Xx92YvQ&list=TLImZCTLGQ
NmEuo_ne_GlOwW4CTBcNGyPZ

MILE THREE
Gung Ho! Turn On the People in Any Organization
Author: Ken Blanchard, Publisher: William Morrow (1987)

MILE SIX
Leadership Lesson from Dancing guy – Derek Sivers
http://www.youtube.com/watch?v=fW8amMCVAJQ

About Bayard Rustin
www.rustin.org

http://en.wikipedia.org/wiki/Midge_Ure

MILE SEVEN
Pygmalion in the classroom By Robert Rosenthal,
Lenore Jacobson in The Urban Review (1968)

MILE THIRTEEN
What Got You Here Won't Get You There: How Successful People
Become Even More Successful.
Author: Marshall Goldsmith, Publisher: Jossey-Bass; (2007).

The Peter Principle
Author: Dr. Laurence J. Peter, Publisher: Bantam (1972).

MILE FOURTEEN
Out of the Crisis. Author: W. Edwards Deming,
Publisher: Massachusetts Institute of Technology (1989).

MILE SEVENTEEN
On the Red Carpet Interview with Sam Mendes
http://www.ontheredcarpet.com/Sam-Mendes:-I-put-everything-I-ever-wanted-into-Skyfall/8881329

MILE TWENTY
Top Ten Mistakes the Bush Administration Is Repeating from Vietnam
Author: Ivan Eland, The Independent Institute (2006)
http://www.independent.org/newsroom/article.asp?id=1694

MILE TWENTY TWO
Military Adage – Proper Prior Preparation Prevents Piss Poor Performance.
History Learning Site – The Roman Army and Warefare.
http://www.historylearningsite.co.uk/roman_army_and_warfare.htm
http://en.wikipedia.org/wiki/Paul_Tergat

MILE TWENTY THREE
Ring Talk - JOE LOUIS SAID: "YOU CAN RUN, BUT YOU CAN'T HIDE" Author Professor Chuck Marbry (2011)
http://ringtalk.com/joe-louis-rocky-marciano-duane-chapman-boxing-muhammad-ali
http://en.wikipedia.org/wiki/Billy_Conn

MILE TWENTY FOUR
Mile run world record progression
http://en.wikipedia.org/wiki/Mile_run_world_record_progression

MILE TWENTY FIVE
You Get Nowt for Being Second
Author: Billy Bremner, Souvenir Press Ltd (1969)

Recommended Further Reading

Throughout the course of my career the following books have helped shape my thinking, provide valuable insights and I would recommend them as further reading for anyone wanting to improve their understanding of Leadership.

Gung Ho! Turn On the People in Any Organization
Author: Ken Blanchard, Publisher: William Morrow (1987)

The 7 Habits of Highly Effective People: Powerful Lessons in Personal Change
Author: Stephen R. Covey, Publisher: Free Press (2004)

The 8th Habit: From Effectiveness to Greatness
Author Stephen R. Covey Publisher: Free Press (2005)

Principle-Centered Leadership
Author: Stephen R. Covey Publisher: Fireside Press; (1992)

Gung Ho! Turn On the People in Any Organization
Author: Ken Blanchard, Publisher: William Morrow (1987)

Leading at a Higher Level, Blanchard on Leadership and Creating High Performing Organizations
Author: Ken Blanchard Publisher: FT Press; 1 edition (2009)

Raving Fans: A Revolutionary Approach To Customer Service
Author: Ken Blanchard
Publisher: William Morrow; 1 edition (1993)

Goals!: How to Get Everything You Want -- Faster Than You Ever Thought Possible
Paperback Author: Brian Tracy
Publisher: BBC Audiobooks America; Abridged edition (2004)

Winning Teams--Winning Cultures
Author: Larry Senn and Jim Hart,
Publisher: Senn Delaney; 2nd edition (2006)

Winning with a Culture of Recognition: Recognition Strategies at the World's Most Admired Companies
Author: Eric Mosley Publisher: Globoforce Limited (2010)

The Five Dysfunctions of a Team: A Leadership Fable
Author: Patrick Lencioni, Publisher: Jossey-Bass; (2002)

Good to Great: Why Some Companies Make the Leap...And Others Don't
Author: Jim Collins, Publisher: HarperBusiness; (2001)

Leadership
Author: Rudolph W. Giuliani and Ken Kurson,
Publisher: Hyperion; (2002)